THE JAPAN BOOK

Kodansha International
Tokyo·New York·London

Geography and Nature

History

Government and Diplomacy

Economy

Society

*Culture
and
Life*

Published by Kodansha International Ltd.
17-14 Otowa 1-chome
Bunkyo-ku, Tokyo 112-8652

First edition, 2002

ISBN4-7700-2847-4

Printed in Japan

Photo credits:
Bon Color Photos Agency Co., Ltd.
Geographic Photo
Haga Library
Kyodo Photo Service

Book design by Parastyle

Contents

Explanatory Notes

Organization
This book is divided into six thematic sections, each containing in-depth entries on specific subjects.

Romanization and Italicization
Japanese words are spelled in this book according to the Hepburn system of romanization used in most English-language publications on Japan. However, macrons differentiating long vowels from short vowels have not been used. Chinese words and names are given in the official *pinyin* system of romanization.

Personal Names
Japanese, Chinese, and Korean personal names are given surname first, the normal order used in those languages (e.g., Kawabata Yasunari rather than Yasunari Kawabata or Kawabata, Yasunari).

Dates
Dates prior to Japan's adoption of the Western calendar on 1 January 1873 have been converted from the old Japanese lunar civil calendar. Every effort has been made to give precise conversions, accounting for the discrepancy between the beginning of the year in the lunar calendar and that in the Western solar calendar. Thus the dates given in this book will sometimes differ from those found in many other reference sources, both Japanese and Western, which frequently assign a date at the beginning or end of the lunar year to the wrong solar year.

The period boundaries used in this book may differ from those found in other reference sources.

Japan is an island nation located in the Pacific Ocean east of the Asian continent. Blessed with diverse natural beauty, most of the land is mountainous and there are many swift-flowing rivers. Separated from each other by mountains and the sea, Japan's many regions over the centuries developed their own characteristic dialects and customs.

Country

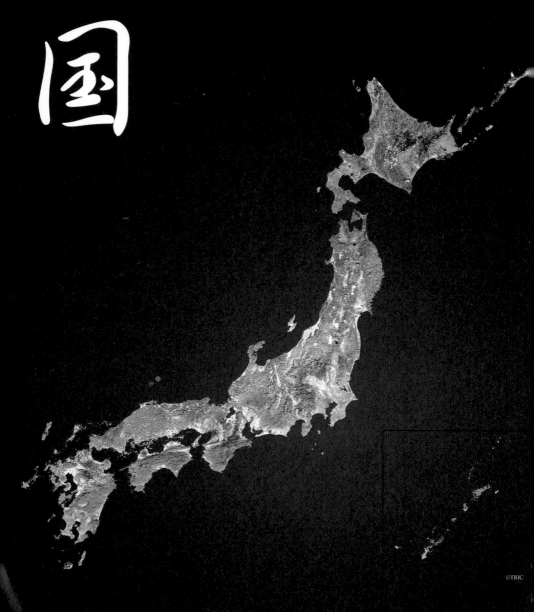

Geography and Nature

Japan experiences four distinct seasons, and from ancient
times its people have found much pleasure in their appreciation
of the characteristic colors of each. Seasonal images play
a central role in much of traditional Japanese poetry,
particularly *haiku*. Contemplation of the colors of the season
—as embodied in innumerable familiar images: a single flower
displayed in the alcove, a flower-petal-shaped slice of raw
fish, a flower-blossom-shaped confection (pictured below)—
has long warmed and calmed hearts and minds.

Land

■Area

Japan (called Nihon or Nippon in Japanese) consists of an archipelago extending approximately from southwest to northeast and ranging from 20°25′ to 45°33′ north latitude. It lies off the east coast of the Asian continent. The total land area is 377,873 square kilometers, which is only slightly larger than that of Finland, Vietnam, or Malaysia and only one twenty-fifth that of the United States. The four major islands of Japan are Hokkaido, Honshu, Shikoku, and Kyushu. The areas of the main geographical divisions of Japan (including offshore islands under their administrative control) are as follows: Hokkaido 83,453 sq km, Honshu 231,078 sq km, Shikoku 18,788 sq km, Kyushu 42,165 sq km, and Okinawa Prefecture 2,271 sq km. Japan set its territorial limit at 12 nautical miles from the coast in 1977.

Note: The northernmost Japanese islands of Kunashiri, Etorofu, the Habomai Islands, and Shikotan were occupied by the Soviet Union after the end of World War II and are still occupied by the Russian Federation today.

■Capital

The capital of Japan is Tokyo, located on the Kanto Plain on the Pacific coast of central Honshu. Tokyo is the site of the Imperial Palace, the Diet, and the Supreme Court. As Japan's economic center, Tokyo hosts the head offices of most large Japanese corporations and media organizations. Area: 2,187 sq km; pop: 12,064,000 (2000).

■Population

At the time of the Meiji Restoration (1868) Japan's population was about 33 million. In 2000 it was 126,926,000, ninth largest in the world. The population density per square kilometer was 340 persons in 2000. The density of the Japanese population per unit area under cultivation is the highest in the world, because over two-thirds of Japan is occupied by mountainous terrain, and alluvial plains occupy only 13 percent.

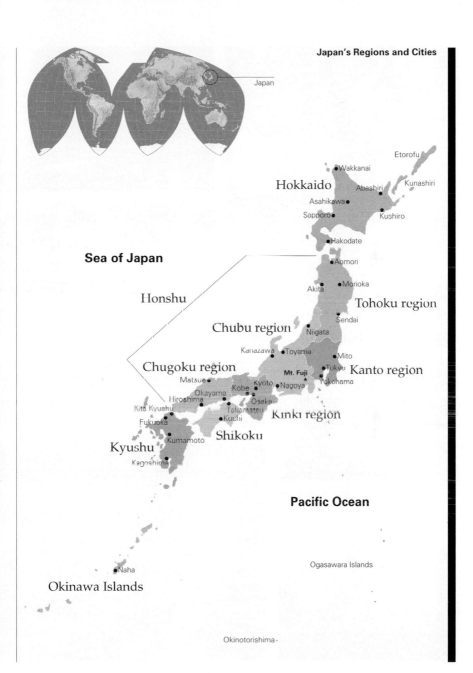

Japan

Etorofu

●Wakkanai

Hokkaido

Abashiri ● Kunashiri

Asahikawa●

Sapporo● Kushiro

●Hakodate

Sea of Japan

●Aomori

Honshu

Akita ● ●Morioka

Tohoku region

Sendai

Chubu region Niigata

Kanazawa ●Toyama

● Mito

Chugoku region **Mt. Fuji** ●Tokyo **Kanto region**

Matsue● ●Yokohama

Okayama● Kyoto ●Nagoya

Hiroshima● Kobe● Osaka

Kita Kyushu● ●Takamatsu

Fukuoka● ●Kochi **Kinki region**

●Kumamoto **Shikoku**

Kyushu

Kagoshima●

Pacific Ocean

●Naha Ogasawara Islands

Okinawa Islands

Okinotorishima·

World Heritage Sites in Japan

As of December 2000, 11 places in Japan had been registered as World Heritage sites. The year of registration is shown in parentheses.

Himeji Castle (1993). Pictured here, at right, is the main donjon.——❷

Horyuji and other temples in the area (1993).——⑧

Part of the island Yakushima (1993). Pictured here is an ancient cryptomeria tree which is thought to be over 3,000 years old.——❶

Shirakami Mountains (1993). Pictured here is a virgin forest of beech trees.——❼

Historic temples and shrines in and around Kyoto (1994).——⑨

Villages of Shirakawa and Gokayama (1995). Pictured here are old farm houses in Shirakawa.——❺

Hiroshima Peace Memorial (1996). Pictured here is the Atomic Bomb Dome.——❻

Itsukushima Shrine (1996).——⑩

Historic temples and shrines in and around Nara (1998).——⑪

Shrines and temples of Nikko (1999). Pictured here is the Yomeimon, the main gate of the Toshogu Shrine at Nikko.——❹

Gusuku (castle) sites and related properties of the Kingdom of Ryukyu (2000). Pictured here is an aerial view of the Shurijo Castle Park in Okinawa.——❸

Japan's National Parks

There were 28 national parks in Japan as of the end of 2001.

Mt. Fuji, the highest mountain in Japan (3,776 m), and Lake Kawaguchi. Part of Fuji-Hakone-Izu National Park.——Ⓐ

The rocky coast of Jodogahama, part of Rikuchu Coast National Park.——Ⓑ

The forested slope of the volcano Daisen, part of Daisen Oki National Park.——Ⓒ

Lake Mashu, part of Akan National Park.——Ⓓ

■**Prefectural System**

After the Meiji Restoration the country was administratively reorganized into a prefectural system and the feudal domains were abolished. At present Japan is administratively divided into 47 prefectures, including 1 *to* (Tokyo To), 1 *do* (Hokkaido), 2 *fu* (Osaka Fu and Kyoto Fu), and 43 *ken*.

Natural Features of Japan

■**Topography**

The chief feature of the Japanese archipelago is its geological instability, including frequent volcanic activity, caused by the 86 active volcanoes, and many earthquakes. Another distinctive characteristic of the topography is the fact that the Japanese archipelago is made up largely of steep mountain districts with very few plains.

■**Climate**

Located in the monsoon zone of the eastern coast of the Asian continent, the most notable features of the climate of the Japanese archipelago are the wide range of yearly temperatures and the large amount of rainfall. However, because of the complexity of the land configuration, there are numerous regional differences throughout the seasons.

Spring: When low-pressure areas pass over the Pacific coast of Japan in March, the temperature rises with each rainfall. When low-pressure areas start to develop over the Sea of Japan, the strong wind from the

Atmospheric Pressure Configuration

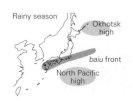

Rainy season

Okhotsk high

baiu front

North Pacific high

Winter

Siberian high

Aleutian low

south called *haru ichiban* (the first tidings of spring) blows over Japan. Spring is blossom time, and cherry-blossom viewing (*hanami*) is a popular pastime.

Summer: The onset of the rainy season (*baiu* or *tsuyu*) takes place around early June. It starts in the southern part of Japan and moves northward. With the end of the rain around 20 July, the Ogasawara air masses blanket Japan, and the weather takes on a summer pattern. The peak of summer is late July, and the summer heat lingers on during August.

Fall: September is the typhoon season. Weather resembling that of the rainy season also occurs because of the autumnal rain fronts. The weather clears in mid-October, and the fall foliage and the first frost appear in northern Japan.

Winter: In December, when the atmospheric pressure configuration has completely changed to the winter pattern, northwest winds bring snow to the mountains and to the plains on the Sea of Japan side, and a dry wind blows on the Pacific Ocean side.

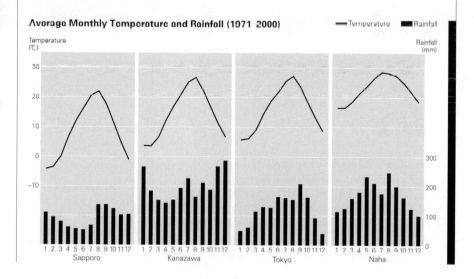

Average Monthly Temperature and Rainfall (1971 2000)

伝

In ancient times Japan did not have a written language. A native Japanese script, called *"kana,"* was born when ideographic characters imported from China were used to represent specific Japanese syllables. The newfound ability to accurately communicate facts and feelings in writing greatly changed the course of Japanese history. This detail from the *Tale of Genji* scrolls, a 12th-century National Treasure, shows a Heian court lady reading aloud to the other ladies.

踊

History

©Tokyo National Museum

Haniwa are unglazed earthenware sculptures that were placed on and around the great mounded tombs (*kofun*) of Japan's rulers during the 4th to 7th centuries. Made in a variety of shapes—from simple cylinders to people, animals, tools, and houses—they provide important clues concerning the lives of the people of the time.

History of Japan

■Prehistoric Period

Archaeologists usually divide the prehistoric phase into four major periods: a long paleolithic preceramic period prior to ca 10,000 BC; the Jomon period (ca 10,000 BC–ca 300 BC), which saw the introduction of ceramics; the Yayoi period (ca 300 BC–ca AD 300), when metals and sedentary agriculture became widespread; and the Kofun period (ca 300–710), age of the great tomb mounds and the beginnings of political centralization.

The first inhabitants of the Japanese islands were paleolithic hunter-gatherers from the continent who used sophisticated stone blades but had no ceramics or settled agriculture. This paleolithic culture persisted until the close of the Pleistocene epoch, about 13,000 years ago, when the Japanese climate ameliorated and sea levels began to rise. In these changing climatic circumstances a new culture began to overlay the older paleolithic culture. This new culture is known as Jomon (literally, "cord marked") from the magnificent pottery that characterized it.

From about 300 BC Jomon culture was overlaid by a distinctly different culture, the Yayoi, characterized by less flamboyant ceramics, a knowledge of bronze and iron technologies, including fine weaponry,

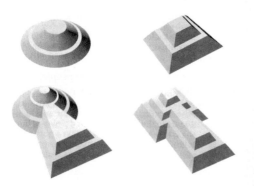

Large tomb mounds, called *kofun*, were built mainly for the ruling elite during the 4th to 7th centuries. They ranged in size from 15 meters in diameter to 32.3 hectares in area; four of the main types are shown here.

and the systematic development of wet-field rice agriculture. These developments laid the basis for the agricultural way of life that profoundly shaped Japanese society into the modern era. They also contributed to greater social stratification.

■Protohistoric Period

Before the close of the Yayoi period, from about the mid-3rd century, clans in the Yamato region (now Nara Prefecture) and other areas of central and western Japan were building tomb mounds for the burial of their chieftains.

By the end of the 7th century, the old clan society was being restructured and Japan was already well on the way to the articulation of a Chinese-inspired centralized imperial administration. The Asuka period (593–710) marks the final phase of this transition between protohistory and history proper. The Asuka period dates from the establishment of the court of Empress Suiko in the Asuka region of Yamato. In 593 Prince Shotoku began to serve as her regent. Buddhism had been introduced to this region in the mid-6th century, and it was here that Prince Shotoku set the country on the course of centralized reform. The Japanese court sponsored Buddhism; built temples, palaces, and capitals after Korean and later Chinese models; began to write histories using Chinese characters; and laid out a blueprint for the *ritsuryo* (legal codes) system.

■Ancient Period

In 710 a magnificent new capital, called Heijokyo and modeled on the Chinese Tang dynasty (618–907) capital at Chang'an, was established at Nara. During the course of the Nara period (710–794) Japan received even more direct cultural and technological influences from China. Buddhism and Confucianism were harnessed to support political authority, and temples were constructed in the capital and in each of the provinces. Centralized administrative systems were instituted. By the closing years of the 8th century, however, the centralized impe-

Major Periods of Japanese History

Western calendar*¹	Periods*²	Major era names*³	Western periodization
	Paleolithic (pre–10,000 BC)		Prehistoric
10,000 BC			
	Jomon (ca 10,000 BC–ca 300 BC)		
300 BC			
	Yayoi (ca 300 BC–ca AD 300)		
AD 300			Protohistoric
400			
500	**Kofun** (Yamato; ca 300–710)		
600		**Taika** (645–650)	
	Asuka (593–710)	**Taiho** (701–704)	
700			
	Nara (710–794)	**Tempyo** (729–749)	Ancient
800			
900		**Jogan** (859–877) **Engi** (901–923)	
1000	**Heian** (794–1185)		
1100			
		Hogen (1156–1159) **Heiji** (1159–1160)	
1200	**Kamakura** (1185–1333) (Kamakura shogunate; 1192–1333)	**Jokyu** (1219–1222)	Medieval
1300			
		Kemmu (1334–1336)	
1400	**Muromachi** (1333–1568) (Muromachi shogunate; 1338–1573) **Northern and Southern Courts** (1336–1392)		
		Onin (1467–1469)	
1500	**Sengoku** (1467–1568)		
	Azuchi-Momoyama (Oda-Toyotomi or Shokuho; 1568–1600)		Early modern
1600		**Bunroku** (1593–1596)	
1700	**Edo** (1600–1868) (Tokugawa shogunate; 1603–1867)	**Genroku** (1688–1704)	
1800		**Bunka** (1804–1818) **Bunsei** (1818–1831)	
1900	**Meiji** (1868–1912)	**Meiji** (1868–1912)	Modern
	Taisho (1912–1926)	**Taisho** (1912–1926)	
	Showa (1926–1989)	**Showa** (1926–1989)	Contemporary
2000	**Heisei** (1989–)	**Heisei** (1989–)	

©Museum of the Imperial Collection, Sannomaru Shozokan

©Imperial Household Agency

©Rinno-ji

*¹ When dates prior to Japan's adoption of the Western calendar on 1 January 1873 were converted from the old Japanese lunar civil calendar, every effort was made to correctly account for the discrepancy between the beginning of the year in the lunar calendar and that in the Western solar calendar. Thus the dates used will sometimes differ from those found in many other reference sources, which frequently assign a date at the beginning or end of the lunar year to the wrong solar year.

*² The period boundaries used here and throughout this book may differ from those found in other reference sources.

*³ Assigned by the imperial court, era names (*nengo*) were adopted in 645 based on a Chinese practice. In the premodern period, era names were changed frequently, sometimes in hopes of bringing about a change of fortune for the country. With the Meiji Restoration of 1868, the present system of using one era name for each imperial reign was adopted. About 250 era names have been used; only major era names are shown in the table.

① The tomb mound that is thought to be the burial place of Emperor Nintoku, who reigned in the first half of the 5th century.

② Prince Shotoku.

③ Emperor Go-Daigo.

④ Tokugawa Ieyasu.

rial administration and public land allotment system were showing signs of strain. Politics in Nara were upset by rivalries among nobles and clerics. In 784 Emperor Kammu decided to make a new start and tried to revive the *ritsuryo* system by moving the capital to a new site. In 794 a new capital, called Heiankyo (literally, "Capital of Peace and Tranquility"), was established where the modern city of Kyoto now stands. This was to serve as the home of the imperial court and the capital of Japan until the 19th century, when the capital was moved to Edo (now Tokyo).

The period from 794 to 1185 is known as the Heian period. It saw the full assimilation of Chinese culture and the flowering of an elegant courtly culture. Politically, however, the imperial court came to be dominated by nobles of the Fujiwara family. In the absence of an effective centralized military system, warrior bands began to assume more power, first in the provinces and then over the court itself when the Taira family seized power in the capital in the mid-12th century.

■Medieval Period

The Taira were overthrown in the Taira-Minamoto War in 1185 by warriors led by Minamoto no Yoritomo, who established a military government, called the Kamakura shogunate, in the small town of Kamakura in eastern Japan in 1192. The court was not displaced by the creation of a military government in Kamakura but its influence steadily weakened. The shogunate assumed control of the administration of justice, the imperial succession, and the defense of the country against the attempted Mongol invasions of Japan in the late 13th century. Headed first by Yoritomo, the Kamakura shogunate was overthrown in 1333 by a coalition led by Emperor Go-Daigo.

Go-Daigo himself was ousted in 1336 by Ashikaga Takauji, who established a new shogunate in Kyoto. After several decades of conflict, the shogunate was put on a firm footing by Ashikaga Yoshimitsu, the third Ashikaga shogun. Later Ashikaga shoguns were less success-

In 1274 and 1281 China's first Mongol emperor, Kublai Khan, sent naval expeditions to invade Japan, but each was repelled with the aid of a fortuitous storm. In this section of the 13th-century *Scrolls of the Mongol Invasion*, a Japanese warrior charges a band of Mongol archers.

©Museum of the Imperial Collection, Sannomaru Shōzōkan

ful in controlling the feudal coalition. Beginning with the Onin War (1467–1477), the country slipped into the century of sporadic civil war known as the Warring States period (Sengoku period; 1467–1568).

■ Early Modern Period

From the mid-16th century, a movement toward national reunification gradually emerged out of the violence of the warring feudal domains and was carried through by three powerful hegemons, Oda Nobunaga, Toyotomi Hideyoshi, and Tokugawa Ieyasu. The short but spectacular epoch during which Nobunaga and Hideyoshi established their military control over the country and began to reshape its feudal institutions is known as the Azuchi-Momoyama period (1568–1600). This was an age of gold, grandeur, and openness to the outside world. After Hideyoshi's death, Tokugawa Ieyasu established a powerful and enduring shogunate in the city of Edo (now Tokyo), ushering in the Edo period (1600–1868) in Japanese history.

Ieyasu's victory gave him preponderant power and allowed him to rearrange the political map of Japan. He established a carefully balanced political structure known as the *bakuhan* (shogunate and domain) system in which the Tokugawa shogunate directly controlled Edo and the heartland of the country while the *daimyo* (military lords) governed the domains. The number of domains varied but during the 18th cen-

Historic Temples and Shrines of Nara and Kyoto

The capital of Japan and home of the imperial court was Nara from 710 to 784 and Kyoto from 794 to 1869. These cities are famous for the many Buddhist temples and Shinto shrines that were established when they served as national capital and that still exist today.

① Kinkakuji (Temple of the Golden Pavilion) in Kyoto.

② The approach to the Kibune Shrine in Kyoto.

③ The main hall of the temple Kiyomizudera in Kyoto.

④ Ginkakuji (Temple of the Silver Pavilion) in Kyoto.

⑤ The five-storied pagoda of the temple Toji in Kyoto.

⑥ Kami-Gamo Sha, one of the two associated Kamo Shrines in Kyoto.

⑦ Sanjusangendo in Kyoto. The 33 bays of this small Buddhist temple contain 1,001 statues of the "Thousand-Armed Kannon."

⑧ The Great Buddha of Nara at the temple Todaiji in Nara.

⑨ The main hall of the temple Toshodaiji in Nara.

tury it stabilized around 260. Ieyasu and his shogunal successors were able to maintain a strong centralized feudal structure by balancing the *daimyo* domains; enforcing status distinctions between warriors (*samurai*), peasants, artisans, and merchants; eradicating Christianity; and controlling contacts with the outside world. This structure was dominated by warriors and relied heavily on the tax yield of the peasants, but it also gave scope to the merchants of Edo, Osaka, Kyoto, and the castle towns to develop commerce and a lively urban culture.

■Modern Period

The Tokugawa system, oppressive as it was in many respects, gave the country more than two centuries of peace and relative seclusion (some access was permitted to Dutch, Chinese, and Koreans) from the outside world (National Seclusion). This was threatened in the 19th century as Russian, British, and American vessels began to probe Asian waters and press for trade with China and Japan. The concession of unequal treaties and the opening of ports after Perry's visit in 1853 set in motion a chain of events that led several powerful domains to use the imperial court to challenge the shogunate, which was overthrown in the Meiji Restoration of 1868. The young warriors who carried through the restoration wanted to preserve, revitalize, and strengthen the country. This process moved ahead rapidly during the course of the Meiji period (1868–1912). Most of the new social, political, and economic institutions created by Japan in its drive to become a modern nation were modeled after those in Western nations. Japan adopted a constitution in 1889, opening the way to parliamentary government. It achieved industrial progress and built up sufficient military power to defeat China in 1895 and Russia in 1905, and to annex Korea in 1910, emerging as the major imperialist power in East Asia.

The Taisho period (1912–1926) was marked by Japan's acceptance as a major power and a period of party government sometimes known as Taisho Democracy. The Showa period (1926–1989) began on a note of optimism but quickly descended into military aggression in China and Japan's departure from the League of Nations. Ultranationalism and political oppression at home eventually led to war with the United States and the Allied powers in Asia and the Pacific.

■Contemporary Era

The defeat of Japan in 1945 under atomic clouds brought the Allied Occupation, demilitarization, dismantling of the old industrial combines, renunciation of divinity by the emperor, a new constitution, democratization, and a new educational system. After a painful period of postwar rehabilitation, the Japanese economy surged ahead from the mid-1950s through the mid-1970s. The Tokyo Olympics in 1964 brought Japan renewed international recognition. The nation's prosperity during this period was based on a consistent stress on economic growth and business-oriented policy making, an emphasis on education, and the frugality, energy, and sustained efforts of the Japanese people. The economy also benefited from the overall global economic expansion generated in the decades after the war as a result of the introduction of free trade principles. In 1968 Japan became the world's second largest economy, and in 1985 it had, for the first time, the largest net external assets in the world. By the 1980s Japan had become the leading manufacturer of cars in the world, and the dominant producer of electronic products.

Since the beginning of the Heisei period in 1989, however, Japan has faced major economic and social challenges. The excesses of the so-called bubble economy of the late 1980s ended in the worst recession of the postwar era. At the same time, Japanese society is facing serious new problems such as a falling birthrate and a rapidly aging population. To deal with these difficult issues, Japan at the beginning of the 21st century is moving forward with reforms to postwar-era practices in all aspects of society, including government, finance, education, and social security.

The new Constitution of Japan was signed on 3 November 1946. Emphasizing democracy, pacifism, and respect for basic human rights, it was enacted to provide a constitutional foundation on which to build a new Japan. Shown here is the part of the original document that has the seal and signature of the Emperor Showa and the signatures of the cabinet ministers.

Law

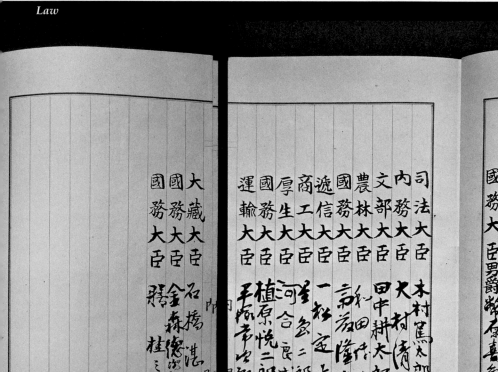

Government and Diplomacy

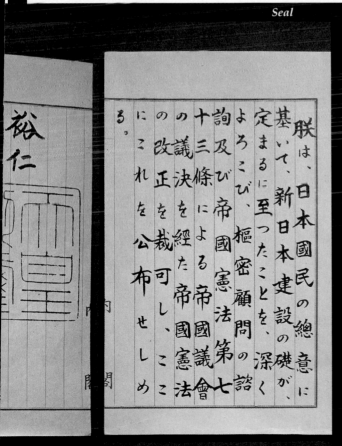

In Japan the parties involved in contracts and other legal agreements affix their seals to the document rather than their signatures. Cases called *inro*, which literally means "seal basket," may have originally been used to carry personal seals, although in the Edo period (1600–1868) they were primarily used for carrying medicine. Worn suspended by a cord and toggle from the *obi* belt, ornate lacquer *inro* such as the example shown here became fashion status symbols for Japanese men in the 18th and 19th centuries.

©Tokyo National Museum

Seal

朕は、日本國民の總意に基いて、新日本建設の礎が、定まるに至つたことを、深くよろこび、樞密顧問の諮詢及び帝國憲法第七十三條による帝國議會の議決を經た帝國憲法の改正を裁可し、ここにこれを公布せしめる。

裕仁

印

Constitution of Japan

The Constitution of Japan, successor to the Constitution of the Empire of Japan (1889; also known as the Meiji Constitution), was promulgated on 3 November 1946 and became effective on 3 May 1947. Consisting of 11 chapters with a total of 103 articles, it is notable for its declaration that sovereignty resides with the people, its assertion of fundamental human rights, and its renunciation of war. A thoroughly democratic document, it revolutionized the political system, which under the Meiji Constitution had been based on the principle that sovereignty resided with the emperor.

■Provisions

The Emperor: Chapter 1, article 1, of the Constitution of Japan declares that "the Emperor shall be the symbol of the State and of the unity of the people, deriving his position from the will of the people with whom resides sovereign power." All acts of the emperor in matters of state require the advice and approval of the cabinet, and the emperor has no "powers related to government." (See Emperor.)

Renunciation of War: Chapter 2, consisting of a single article, article 9, states that the Japanese people "forever renounce war" and that, to accomplish this aim, "land, sea, and air forces, as well as other war potential, will never be maintained."

The Bill of Rights: Chapter 3 enumerates the rights and duties of the people, such as freedom of speech. Discrimination "in political, economic or social relations because of race, creed, sex, social status or family origin" is forbidden. The people have the right to maintain "minimum standards of wholesome and cultured living," and the state is expected to promote social welfare and security and public health. The right to own property is declared inviolable.

The National Legislature: Chapter 4 declares that the Diet is "the highest organ of state power" and "the sole law-making organ of the

State." (See Diet.)

The Cabinet: Chapter 5 concerns the cabinet. The prime minister is designated by a resolution of the Diet, and he or she selects and dismisses the other cabinet members. The cabinet is collectively responsible to the Diet. If the House of Representatives passes a resolution of no confidence (or rejects a resolution of confidence) in the cabinet, either the cabinet must resign en masse or the House of Representatives must be dissolved within 10 days. (See Executive Branch of the Government.)

The Courts: The judiciary is described in chapter 6 of the constitution. The Japanese Supreme Court is the court of last resort with power to determine the constitutionality of legislation and government acts. (See Judicial System.)

Finance: Chapter 7 concerns the government's finances, and establishes the Diet's control over the imposing of taxes and the expenditure of funds.

Local Government: Chapter 8 defines the "principle of local autonomy" for local public entities. (See Local Government.)

Emperor

Under the Constitution of Japan the emperor is "the symbol of the State and of the unity of the people, deriving his position from the will of the people with whom resides sovereign power." He has no powers related to government. All acts by the emperor in matters of state are merely formal and ceremonial functions, requiring the advice and approval of the cabinet. In January 1989, Emperor Akihito became the first emperor to succeed to the throne under the present constitution.

■Emperor Akihito

The present emperor and 125th sovereign in the traditional count (which includes several legendary emperors). Born in 1933 as the eldest son of Emperor Showa and Empress Kojun. In 1952 he entered the Faculty of Political Science and Economics at Gakushuin University, and in November of that year the Ceremony of Coming-of-Age and the investiture as crown prince were conducted. He completed his course of studies at Gakushuin University in March 1956. In April 1959 Crown Prince Akihito married Shoda Michiko.

On 7 January 1989 he became Emperor Akihito, succeeding to the throne after his father's death. The following day the formal reign title Heisei ("Establishing Peace") was adopted.

Like his father, Emperor Akihito is known as a scholar of marine biology and ichthyology and for his research into the fishes of the family Gobiidae. He also enjoys sports and is a lover of music, playing cello in impromptu performances with other members of the royal family. He and Empress Michiko have three children: Crown Prince Naruhito, Prince Akishino, and Princess Sayako.

■Empress Michiko

Wife of Emperor Akihito. Born in 1934 as the eldest daughter of Shoda Hidesaburo, a businessman, and his wife Fumiko. She is a grad-

©Imperial Household Agency

The imperial family is shown here in a December 2001 photograph. Standing (from left to right): Princess Kako, Prince Akishino, Princess Mako, Princess Akishino, and Princess Sayako; sitting: Crown Princess Masako, Princess Aiko, Emperor Akihito, Empress Michiko, and Crown Prince Naruhito.

uate of the University of the Sacred Heart in Tokyo. In April 1959 she married then crown prince Akihito. Her marriage to Crown Prince Akihito was broadly welcomed by the Japanese people. On 7 January 1989 she became empress upon her husband's ascension to the throne as Emperor Akihito. Empress Michiko maintains a lively interest in literature, arts, and music and serves as honorary president of the Japan Red Cross Society.

■**Crown Prince Naruhito**

Born in 1960 as the eldest son of Emperor Akihito and Empress Michiko. The crown prince graduated from Gakushuin University in 1982 and completed his initial coursework for the doctorate in history there in 1988. From 1983 to 1985 he studied at Merton College, Oxford University, where he conducted research into river transportation on the Thames during the 18th century. He celebrated the Ceremony of Investiture as crown prince on 23 February 1991. In June 1993 Crown Prince Naruhito married Owada Masako. Their first child, Princess Aiko, was born on 1 December 2001.

■**Crown Princess Masako**

Wife of Crown Prince Naruhito. Born in 1963 as the eldest daughter of Owada Hisashi, a diplomat, and his wife Yumiko. She married the crown prince in June 1993. She graduated from Harvard University in the United States with a major in economics and then did further study at the University of Tokyo. She joined the Ministry of Foreign Affairs in April 1987. Beginning in the summer of 1988 she spent two years studying at Balliol College, Oxford University.

National Flag

The national flag of Japan has a crimson disc, symbolizing the sun, in the center of a white field. It is known as the Hinomaru (literally, "sun disc"). The Tokugawa shogunate (1603–1867) adopted the flag for its ships in the early 1600s. In 1870 the Meiji government officially designated it for use on Japanese merchant and naval ships. Acknowledging its long use as the flag symbolizing Japan, the Hinomaru was officially designated the national flag in 1999 under the Law Concerning the National Flag and National Anthem.

National Anthem

The national anthem is "Kimigayo." The words of the song are taken from an ancient poem which is found in such anthologies as the 10th-century *Kokin wakashu* and the 11th-century *Wakan roeishu*. The author is unknown. The government interpretation of the meaning of the anthem was presented by Prime Minister Obuchi Keizo at a 1999 Diet session: "*Kimi* in 'Kimigayo,' under the current Constitution of Japan, indicates the Emperor, who is the symbol of the State and of the unity of the people, deriving his position from the will of the people with whom resides sovereign power; 'Kimigayo' as a whole depicts the state of being of our country, which has the Emperor—deriving his position from the will of the people with whom resides sovereign power—as the

The words and music for "Kimigayo," Japan's national anthem.

symbol of itself and of the unity of the people; and it is appropriate to interpret the words of the anthem as praying for the lasting prosperity and peace of our country."

The tune was composed by Hayashi Hiromori in 1880. In 1893 the Ministry of Education made it the ceremonial song to be sung in elementary schools on national holidays. Soon it was sung at state ceremonies and sports events. Popularly identified as the national anthem for many years, "Kimigayo" was officially designated the national anthem in 1999 under the Law Concerning the National Flag and National Anthem.

Diet

The legislative branch of the Japanese government. According to the Constitution of Japan, the Diet is "the highest organ of state power" and "the sole law-making organ of the State." The Diet consists of two chambers: the House of Representatives, or lower house, and the House of Councillors, or upper house. For the 480 members of the lower house, the term of office is four years unless the house is dissolved before the term elapses. Half of the 242 representatives in the upper house are elected to a six-year term of office every three years. Three categories of Diet sessions are held: ordinary, extraordinary, and special sessions.

The prime minister and a majority of the cabinet ministers are required to be members of the Diet and, "in the exercise of executive power, shall be collectively responsible to the Diet." The right of the cabinet to dissolve the House of Representatives is balanced against the right of that house to pass a resolution of non-confidence in the cabinet.

The House of Representatives and the House of Councillors share legislative power; however, the lower house has authority in three

Completed in 1936, the Diet Building is located in central Tokyo (Nagatacho district). Shown here are the building's main entrance and central tower.

Postwar Political Parties

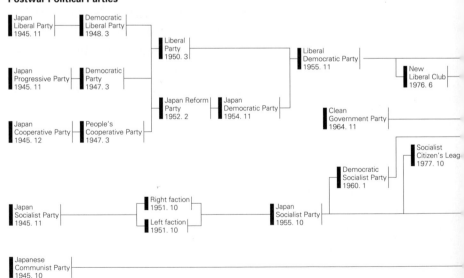

important areas: the budget, treaty ratification, and selection of the prime minister. Also, in all fields of legislation, the lower house can override the upper house by a two-thirds vote.

Political Parties

For most of the postwar period Japanese politics were dominated by the Liberal Democratic Party (LDP) and the Japan Socialist Party (now the Social Democratic Party), both formed in 1955. This "1955 regime" continued until 1993. In July 1993 the LDP lost its parliamentary major-ity, and its administration was subsequently replaced by an eight-party non-LDP coalition. This marked the end of the 1955 regime. In December 1994 most of the parties that had been represented in the 1993 eight-party coalition cabinet joined together to form the New

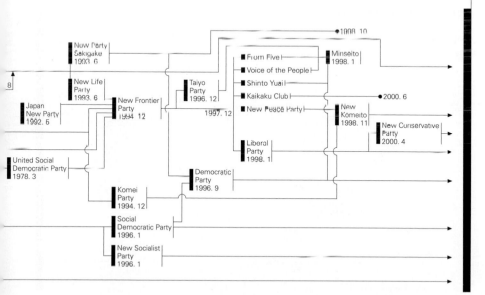

Frontier Party. In September 1996 a large number of Diet members from the New Party Sakigake and the Social Democratic Party left their parties to establish the Democratic Party. The New Frontier Party was disbanded in December 1997. This resulted in the formation of a new Liberal Party and five other smaller parties. Some of these smaller parties later joined the Democratic Party, which became Japan's second largest party following the LDP.

As of January 2002, in the House of Representatives (480 seats total) the number of seats held by the major parties was LDP, 242; Democratic Party, 125; New Komeito, 31; Liberal Party, 22; Japanese Communist Party, 20; Social Democratic Party, 19; and New Conservative Party, 7; and in the House of Councillors (247 seats total) it was LDP, 111; Democratic Party, 57; New Komeito, 24; Japanese Communist Party, 20; Liberal Party, 8; Social Democratic Party, 7; and New Conservative Party, 5.

Diet Political Strength (January 2002)

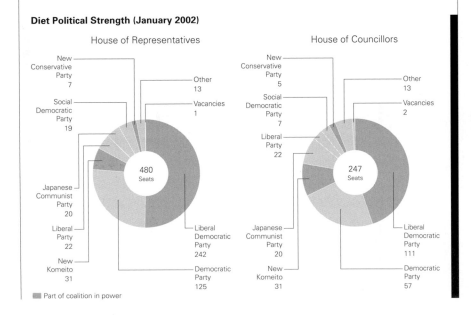

Members of the House of Representatives are shown here in the main chamber voting on a bill in October 2000.

The major political parties in Japan now are the Liberal Democratic Party, the Democratic Party, the New Komeito, the Liberal Party, the Japanese Communist Party, and the Social Democratic Party.

Elections

Japan has had a national election system since the promulgation of the Constitution of the Empire of Japan on 11 February 1889. The extension of the franchise, limited at first to a small proportion of the adult male population, took place gradually, culminating in the adoption of universal suffrage shortly after the end of World War II.

■Current Practices

The election system was given its present form by the Public Office Election Law of April 1950. All Japanese citizens are eligible to vote if they have reached the age of 20 and have met a three-month residency requirement (for voting in local elections). Candidates for political office must meet the stated age requirement for each office. Members of

Organization of the Cabinet

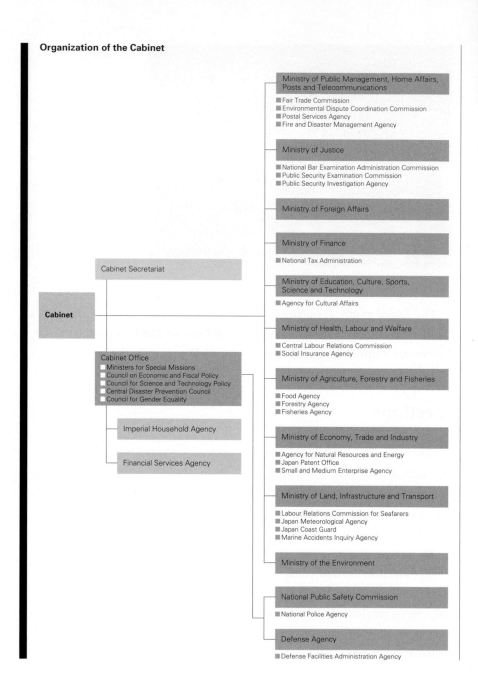

Cabinet

Cabinet Secretariat

Cabinet Office
- Ministers for Special Missions
- Council on Economic and Fiscal Policy
- Council for Science and Technology Policy
- Central Disaster Prevention Council
- Council for Gender Equality

Imperial Household Agency

Financial Services Agency

Ministry of Public Management, Home Affairs, Posts and Telecommunications
- Fair Trade Commission
- Environmental Dispute Coordination Commission
- Postal Services Agency
- Fire and Disaster Management Agency

Ministry of Justice
- National Bar Examination Administration Commission
- Public Security Examination Commission
- Public Security Investigation Agency

Ministry of Foreign Affairs

Ministry of Finance
- National Tax Administration

Ministry of Education, Culture, Sports, Science and Technology
- Agency for Cultural Affairs

Ministry of Health, Labour and Welfare
- Central Labour Relations Commission
- Social Insurance Agency

Ministry of Agriculture, Forestry and Fisheries
- Food Agency
- Forestry Agency
- Fisheries Agency

Ministry of Economy, Trade and Industry
- Agency for Natural Resources and Energy
- Japan Patent Office
- Small and Medium Enterprise Agency

Ministry of Land, Infrastructure and Transport
- Labour Relations Commission for Seafarers
- Japan Meteorological Agency
- Japan Coast Guard
- Marine Accidents Inquiry Agency

Ministry of the Environment

National Public Safety Commission
- National Police Agency

Defense Agency
- Defense Facilities Administration Agency

the House of Representatives and of prefectural and local assemblies must be at least 25 years old. Members of the House of Councillors and prefectural governors must be at least 30.

Under current election laws, members of all legislative bodies, including both houses of the Diet and prefectural, city, town, and village assemblies, are selected by popular vote. Political executives, including prefectural governors and mayors or other chief officials of local governments, are also chosen in popular elections. The prime minister, who is elected by the Diet, is the only political executive not chosen by direct popular vote. House of Councillors members are elected to six-year terms, with elections being held every three years. In 2001 the total number of members was reduced from 252 to 247, and in 2004 it is to be further reduced to 242. In the House of Representatives, the 480 members are elected to four-year terms, typically in elections held irregularly after the dissolution of the House. Of these 480, 300 are elected from single-seat constituencies, and 180 are elected under a proportional representation system. Elections are held every four years for most prefectural and local executive offices and assemblies.

Executive Branch of the Government

The executive branch of the Japanese government consists of the cabinet and the organizations under its control and jurisdiction. According to the Constitution of Japan, the executive power is vested in the cabinet, which consists of the prime minister and ministers of state and is collectively responsible to the Diet, the highest organ of the state. The prime minister is designated by the Diet from among its members and formally appointed by the emperor. He appoints or dismisses the ministers of state, more than half of whom must be Diet members. The prime minister, representing the cabinet, submits bills to the Diet, supervises and controls the executive branch, and reports on national and foreign affairs to the Diet. The cabinet is charged with administration of laws, preparation of the annual budget, conduct of foreign relations and conclusion of treaties, and administration of the civil service.

Under the laws enacted in 1998 and 1999 concerning administrative reform of the central government, in January 2001 the number of ministries and agencies headed by a minister of state was reduced from 22 (12 ministries plus 9 agencies and the National Public Safety Commission) to 12 (10 ministries plus the Defense Agency and the National Public Safety Commission).

Local Government

The new Constitution of Japan (promulgated in 1946) in essence guaranteed the decentralization of political authority by confirming the "principle of local autonomy" and by establishing such basic features of the new system as the separation of local from national administration and the direct popular election of prefectural governors and of mayors, as well as local assemblies. Japan has 47 prefectures and a total of approximately 3,200 cities, towns, and villages.

Beginning in the mid-1950s, local governments became participants in the national drive for economic growth, but by the late 1960s and early 1970s, many local governments began reordering their priorities. Economic growth encouraged a rapid urbanization of the population, and new urban problems such as pollution-related diseases, traffic congestion, and uncontrolled urban sprawl proliferated.

The intensity of such problems resulted in substantial grass-roots protests and efforts by citizens to seek ameliorative policies from local governments. As a result, local priorities diverged significantly from national ones and contributed to the eventual shift in national priorities from unrestricted economic growth to establishing a higher quality of life.

Moreover, government reform efforts of the late 1970s and early 1980s led to an increased reliance on local authorities for the implementation of national social and environmental programs. The Decentralization Promotion Law was enacted in 1995 and led to creation of the Plan for Promoting Decentralization by the cabinet in 1998 and to the passing of the Law for Amendment of Laws Related to the Promotion of Decentralization in 1999. This law clarifies the scope of central and local government roles and responsibilities, and reduces central government procedural requirements for, and participation in, local government affairs to the minimum level necessary. In order to strengthen administrative and financial resources at the local level, and thereby help local government better handle delegated authority and deal with social problems such as population aging and waste disposal, the national government is promoting the consolidation of cities, towns, and villages into larger units.

Judicial System

The Constitution of Japan (art. 76) provides that "the whole judicial power is vested in a Supreme Court and in such inferior courts as are established by law." All courts on all levels are parts of a single system under the sole and complete administration of the Supreme Court. A jury system does not exist.

The structure of the judicial system is as follows: the Supreme Court; 8 high courts in the eight principal geographical subdivisions of the country; 50 district courts in the principal administrative units; 50 family courts; and 438 summary courts located throughout the country. The Diet as the sole law-making organ can change the organization of the courts by passing the necessary legislation, but the administration of the court system remains constitutionally vested in the Supreme Court.

The Supreme Court is headed by the chief justice, who is appointed by the emperor after designation by the cabinet. The other 14 justices are appointed by the cabinet. The court is organized into a grand bench consisting of all 15 justices and three petty benches of 5 justices each. All cases before the Supreme Court are appeals; it possesses original jurisdiction over no cases. The constitution (art. 81) also provides that the Supreme Court is the court of last resort "with power to determine the constitutionality of any law, order, regulation or official act."

The high courts are essentially appellate courts. They are courts of first instance for the crimes of insurrection, preparation for or plotting of insurrection, and of assistance in the acts enumerated.

District courts have original jurisdiction over most cases, with the exception of offenses carrying minor punishment and a few others reserved for other courts. In addition, they are courts of appeal for actions taken by the summary courts. Family courts came into exis-

The Supreme Court Building, located in Chiyoda Ward, Tokyo.

tence in 1949. They have jurisdiction over such matters as juvenile crime (the age of majority being 20), problems of minors, divorce, and disputes over family property. Summary courts have jurisdiction over minor cases involving ¥900,000 or less in claims or fines or offenses carrying lighter punishments.

International Relations

In the last decade of the 20th century, the world was shaken by major upheavals such as the end of the Cold War, acceleration of economic globalization, and revolutionary advances in information technology. With the international community facing new waves of change in the 21st century, interdependence between countries can only continue to increase. To address the many growing problems that transcend national boundaries—security issues, terrorism, economic issues, environmental damage, illegal drugs, refugees, etc.—the extensive cooperation of all countries involved is becoming increasingly critical. While effectively addressing the many changes taking place, Japan's foreign policy in the new century seeks to actively promote the security

©Kyodo

Final meeting of the heads of state attending the G8 summit meeting held in Okinawa in July 2000.

and prosperity of the entire international community, in the recognition that this is inseparable from the security and prosperity of Japan itself.

Japan's close ties with the United States have been a cornerstone of its foreign policy in the postwar era, and this relationship is further strengthened by Japan-U.S. security arrangements (see National Defense). Japan continues to promote further cooperation with neighboring countries such as Russia, China, and the Republic of Korea, and it is working together closely with the Republic of Korea and the United States to improve relations with North Korea. Strong efforts are also being made to strengthen relations with the member states of the Association of Southeast Asian Nations (ASEAN) and the countries of Oceania, and to promote regional cooperation through entities such as the Asia-Pacific Economic Cooperation Forum (APEC), the ASEAN Regional Forum (ARF), and the Asia-Euro Meeting (ASEM).

Since its admission to the United Nations in 1956, Japan has regarded its commitment to the United Nations as one of the main pillars of its foreign policy. Japan is contributing to the resolution of regional disputes through personnel and monetary support provided to United Nations peacekeeping operations and other international efforts. It is also actively supporting international endeavors to fight terrorism and to solve problems in areas such as the environment, illegal drugs, and population growth. The significance of economic issues as a component of international relations has increased significantly in recent years, making economic stability a critical issue in Japanese diplomacy. Recognizing the responsibilities that result from having the world's second largest economy, Japan is working to promote healthy economic development worldwide through organizations such as the IMF, the WTO, and the OECD, and it is also providing technical and financial assistance to developing countries via an official development assistance (ODA) program. In recent years Japan has been making efforts to expand its human resource contribution by, for example, dispatching personnel in Japan Disaster Relief Teams and election-monitoring teams. (See Official Development Assistance.)

Relations with the United States: Bilateral security arrangements and economic ties have formed the core of Japan's postwar relationship with the United States, but the two countries also cooperate extensively in multilateral efforts to solve global problems. In order to update Japan-U.S. security arrangements to reflect the realities of the post–Cold War world, new Guidelines for Japan-U.S. Defense Cooperation were issued in 1997, and laws related to these guidelines were enacted in 1999. This has put the security relationship between the two countries on a stable footing.

On the economic side of the relationship, the United States is the number one destination for Japan's exports and the number one source for its imports. Japan's share in the U.S. trade deficit, which exceeded 60 percent in the early 1990s, dropped to about 20 percent for 2000. This is about the same share as that of China. Against this backdrop, today trade friction between the two countries escalates into a major political issue much less often than during certain periods in the past. In recent trade talks between Japan and the United States, both governments have been promoting deregulation measures under the Enhanced Initiative on Deregulation and Competition Policy.

Relations with China: Japan established diplomatic relations with the People's Republic of China in 1972. Economic relations developed rapidly after that, and today Japan is China's largest trading partner while China is Japan's second largest trading partner. In support of China's reform and open policy, Japan is currently providing economic assistance. The increase in high-level government contact in recent years is helping to deepen mutual understanding between the two governments.

Relations with the Republic of Korea (ROK) and North Korea: The Treaty on Basic Relations between Japan and the Republic of Korea, which provided for diplomatic and consular relations between the two countries, was concluded in 1965.

The 1998 visit to Japan by President Kim Dae Jung of the ROK and the 1999 visit to the ROK by Prime Minister Obuchi Keizo of Japan have helped the two countries to move into a new future-oriented relationship no longer focused on past history. In the 21st century Japan and the ROK will be further strengthening relations through a variety of means, including the holding of the "Year of Japan-ROK National Exchange in 2002," which is also the year of the joint hosting of the Soccer World Cup.

As of 2001 Japan has not established diplomatic relations with North Korea. It is continuing to pursue talks with North Korea in an effort to normalize relations.

Relations with Russia: The first contacts between Japanese and Russians occured in the late 17th century. Japan and Russia first established diplomatic relations in 1855. After the end of World War II, however, the Soviet Union occupied the inherently Japanese territories of Etorofu, Kunashiri, Shikotan, and the Habomai Islands (the Northern Territories). Because of this territorial dispute, no peace treaty was concluded between Japan and the Soviet Union.

©Kyodo

Prime Minister Koizumi Jun'ichiro of Japan (right) and President Kim Dae Jung of the Republic of Korea are shown here at a meeting in Seoul in October 2001.

With the demise of the Soviet Union in 1991 and the emergence of the Russian Federation, Japan-Russia relations entered a new era. In 1993, Prime Minister Hosokawa of Japan and President Yeltsin of Russia signed the Tokyo Declaration, in which they stressed the importance of the early conclusion of a peace treaty through the solution of the territorial dispute.

Since then, Japan and Russia have repeatedly reaffirmed their intention to advance bilateral relations based on this declaration. Especially in recent years, a number of meetings at the leader level have been held with the goal of concluding a peace treaty and promoting ties in economic, cultural, and many other areas.

■United Nations and Japan

Japan was admitted to the United Nations on 18 December 1956, and its foreign policy has since then included commitment to the United Nations as one of its main pillars. Since its admission Japan has been elected to the UN Security Council as a nonpermanent (two-year-term) member eight times, and since 1960 it has been a regular member of the Economic and Social Council. In 2000, Japan's contribution to the UN ordinary budget was 20.6 percent. Since 1986 Japan's contribution has been the second largest, behind the United States.

Japan works for international peace and security through participation in United Nations peacekeeping operations, United Nations and other international efforts for conflict prevention, and active promotion of arms control and non-proliferation. With the enactment of the International Peace Cooperation Law in 1992, Japan started to send its Self-Defense Forces personnel to United Nations peacekeeping operations, making its participation in such United Nations operations one of its significant means of contribution to international peace and security. Japan's international cooperation under the United Nations framework is pursued in a wide range of other areas including assistance for economic and social development of developing countries;

Ogata Sadako (right) served as the United Nations high commissioner for refugees from 1991 to 2000. She is shown here visiting a camp for Mozambique refugees in South Africa.

preservation of the environment; protection of human rights; refugee assistance; the tackling of such global problems threatening human security as small arms and light weapons, anti-personnel landmines, illegal drug trafficking, transnational organized crime, and HIV/AIDS and other infectious diseases; and promotion of international cultural exchange.

With the greater expectations placed on the United Nations in the post-Cold War world, Japan advocates the need to reform the organization to equip it with the power and capacity to effectively respond to the new reality. Japan considers that such reform should include the improvement of the composition and functioning of the Security Council, the adoption of a new development strategy and better coordination of United Nations development activities, and the financial reform of the organization.

■Official Development Assistance

Japan's official development assistance (ODA) includes grant aid, technical assistance, loan aid, and financial support contributed to international organizations engaged in development and relief work.

With an outlay of U.S. $15.32 billion in foreign aid in 1999, Japan was, for the ninth year in a row, the world's largest aid donor, as measured by the disbursement of ODA by the industrial countries represented in the Development Assistance Committee (DAC) of the Organization for Economic Cooperation and Development (OECD). However, measured as a percentage of gross national product (GNP), Japanese aid ranked 7th among the 22 DAC nations at 0.35 percent, as compared to the DAC average value of 0.24.

In 1999, 63.2 percent of Japanese bilateral ODA went to Asia, 9.5 percent to Africa, 7.8 percent to Central and South America, and 5.2 percent to the Middle East. While in absolute monetary terms the amount of Japan's grant aid in the 1998/99 period was the second largest, behind the United States, the grant aid share (i.e., the percentage of funds provided without the need for repayment) of Japan's total ODA averaged 45.4 percent, the lowest level among the 22 DAC countries.

Japan implements its ODA in accordance with the ODA Charter adopted by the cabinet in 1992. This charter sets forth four guiding principles: (1) the pursuit of environmental conservation and development in tandem, (2) the avoidance of the use of ODA for military purposes or for aggravation of international conflicts, (3) monitoring of recipient countries' military expenditures, their development and production of weapons of mass destruction and missiles and their arms

©JICA

©JICA

Left: A Japanese technician providing guidance at an automobile repair facility in Tanzania.
Right: A Japanese nurse giving instructions for the care of a premature baby in Senegal.

trade, and (4) monitoring of their efforts for promoting democratization and introduction of a market-oriented economy and their human rights situation.

The Medium-Term Policy on Official Development Assistance, which was published by the Japanese government in 1999, sets forth guidelines for Japanese ODA over the next five years. Key development issues addressed include the placement of heightened priority on: (1) support for poverty alleviation programs and social development, (2) support for the economic and social infrastructure, (3) human resources development and intellectual support, (4) responding to global issues, (5) support for overcoming the Asian currency and economic crisis and promotion of economic structural reform, (6) conflict, disaster, and development, and (7) responding to issues of debt relief. The global issues include the environment, population, AIDS, food, energy, and drug abuse. Concerning the methods to be used in providing aid, the policy covers support for nongovernmental organization (NGO) aid activities and utilization of NGO personnel resources and expertise, and it also considers the issue of coordination with other donor countries and international organizations.

Geographical Distribution of Japan's Bilateral ODA

(net disbursement basis; in millions of U.S. dollars)

Region	1980		1990		1995		1997		1999	
Asia	1,383	(70.5)	4,117	(59.3)	5,745	(54.4)	3,076	(46.5)	6,631	(63.2)
Northeast Asia	82	(4.2)	835	(12.0)	1,606	(15.2)	530	(8.0)	1,282	(12.2)
Southeast Asia	861	(43.9)	2,379	(34.3)	2,592	(24.6)	1,416	(21.4)	3,921	(37.3)
Southwest Asia	435	(22.2)	898	(12.9)	1,435	(13.6)	964	(14.6)	1,168	(11.1)
Central Asia					67	(0.6)	145	(2.2)	215	(2.0)
Caucasus					0	(0.0)	12	(0.2)	24	(0.2)
Other regions	5	(0.3)	4	(0.1)	44	(0.4)	9	(0.1)	21	(0.2)
Middle East	204	(10.4)	705	(10.2)	721	(6.8)	513	(7.8)	544	(5.2)
Africa	223	(11.4)	792	(11.4)	1,333	(12.6)	803	(12.1)	995	(9.5)
Latin America	118	(6.0)	561	(8.1)	1,142	(10.8)	715	(10.8)	814	(7.8)
Oceania	12	(0.6)	114	(1.6)	160	(1.5)	159	(2.4)	138	(1.9)
Europe	-2	(-)	158	(2.3)	153	(1.4)	134	(2.0)	151	(1.4)
(Eastern Europe)			153	(2.2)	138	(1.3)	54	(0.8)	18	(0.2)
Unspecified	23	(1.2)	494	(7.1)	1,303	(12.3)	1,213	(18.3)	1,225	(11.7)
Total	1,961	(100.0)	6,941	(100.0)	10,557	(100.0)	6,613	(100.0)	10,498	(100.0)

Source: Ministry of Foreign Affairs.

The administration of official Japanese aid programs and policies rests with a number of government ministries and agencies, with the Ministry of Foreign Affairs functioning as a coordinator. They are backed up by two government-funded institutions, the Japan Bank for International Cooperation (JBIC) and the Japan International Cooperation Agency (JICA), which oversee the disbursement of soft loans, export credits, technical assistance, and grant aid. There is no central aid agency as in some other donor countries.

Tokyo International Conference on African Development (TICAD): The first TICAD was held on Japan's initiative in 1993, and TICAD II was convened in Tokyo in 1998. The second conference resulted in the adoption of the Tokyo Agenda for Action, which defines specific strategies for action in the overall fields of social development and poverty reduction, economic development, and basic foundations for development. In conjunction with TICAD II, Japan announced a new assistance program for Africa that included, for example, the providing of ¥90 billion in grant aid over a five-year period for projects in education, health and medical care, and water supply.

■International Cultural Exchange

Between the opening of Japan to foreign contact in the late 19th century and World War I, Japan's international cultural relations stressed the importation of Western culture rather than the introduction abroad of its own culture. Following World War I, the importance of promoting international understanding of Japan through cultural exchange was recognized, and in 1934 the Society for International Cultural Relations was established.

In the period of recovery following World War II, there was little Japanese involvement in international cultural exchange. Rapid economic growth in the 1960s and increased visibility of Japan in the international community, however, prompted greater interest in Japanese culture and society among countries overseas. With the aim of conducting Japan's international cultural relations on a more systematic basis, the Japanese government created a new cultural exchange organization, the Japan Foundation, in 1972.

Japan's international cultural exchange activities are handled mainly by the Ministry of Foreign Affairs, the Ministry of Education, Culture, Sports, Science and Technology, and two public organizations attached to these ministries: the Japan Foundation and the Japan Society for the Promotion of Science. Among the programs administered by these governmental and semigovernmental organizations are educational exchange; academic exchange, including promotion of Japanese language teaching in foreign countries; artistic exchange; cultural materials exchange; and multilateral cultural cooperation, including cooperation with UNESCO and other international organizations.

Private organizations, such as the International House of Japan and the Toyota Foundation, and local governments and citizens' groups are promoting cultural exchange to address issues such as development aid to the Third World, environmental protection, and international peace. In addition, in recent years there has been an increase in the number of major cultural events held in order to provide a comprehensive introduction to Japanese culture.

National Security

Japan's security policy rests on three major pillars: (1) firmly maintaining Japan-U.S. security arrangements; (2) building up Japan's defense capabilities on an appropriate scale based on the National Defense Program Outline; and (3) diplomatic efforts to ensure international peace and security.

■Japan-U.S. Security Arrangements

The original Japan–United States security treaty was signed in

September 1951 and the current treaty, named the Treaty of Mutual Cooperation and Security between Japan and the United States of America, was signed in January 1960. This treaty and its related arrangements not only secure the U.S. presence and involvement in the Asia-Pacific region, where instability and uncertainty still exist, but also form a political foundation for wide-ranging Japan-U.S. cooperative relations in the international community. The Japan-U.S. Joint Declaration on Security, issued in April 1996, reconfirmed that the Japan-U.S. security relationship remains the cornerstone for achieving common security objectives, and for maintaining a stable and prosperous environment in the Asia-Pacific region.

Guidelines for Japan-U.S. Defense Cooperation: To facilitate the effective functioning of the security treaty in effect between Japan and the United States, in 1978 detailed provisions for military cooperation between the two countries were set forth in the Guidelines for Japan-U.S. Defense Cooperation. In order to better reflect the changing international environment in the post–Cold War world, new guidelines were issued in 1997. The new guidelines cover cooperation between Japan and the United States under "normal circumstances" and during contingencies. Included for the first time is cooperation in situations in

©Kyodo

©Defense Agency

Left: Prime Minister Hashimoto Ryutaro of Japan (right) and President William Clinton of the United States at the announcement of the Japan-U.S. Joint Declaration on Security in April 1996.
Right: Troops of the Ground Self-Defense Force marching in an inspection parade in 1998.

Defense-Related Expenditures

	Amount (in trillions of yen)	Percent of GNP or GDP (from 1995)	Percent of national budget
1955	1,349	1.785	13.6
1965	3,014	1.070	8.2
1975	13,273	0.837	6.2
1985	31,371	0.997	6.0
1990	41,593	0.961	6.3
1995	47,236	0.959	6.7
2000	49,218	0.987	5.8

Source: Defense Agency.

areas surrounding Japan that will have an important influence on Japan's peace and security. In order to provide a legal basis for the domestic mechanisms necessary to ensure the effectiveness of the new guidelines, in 1999 the Diet approved: (1) the Law Concerning Measures to Ensure the Peace and Security of Japan in Situations in Areas Surrounding Japan; (2) a bill to amend the Self-Defense Forces Law; and (3) an agreement amending the Japan-U.S. agreement covering reciprocal provision of logistic support, supplies, and services between the Self-Defense Forces of Japan and the Armed Forces of the United States. In addition, in 2000 the Diet approved the Law Concerning the Conduct of Ship Inspection Operations in Situations in Areas Surrounding Japan.

■National Defense Program Outline

The National Defense Program Outline is a policy guideline stipulating the basic nature of Japan's defense policy and specific goals for the level of defense capability it should possess. Japan's three Self-Defense Forces—the Ground Self-Defense Force, the Maritime Self-Defense Force, and the Air Self-Defense Force—are managed and operated in accordance with the provisions of this outline.

The first such outline, established by the Miki Takeo cabinet in 1976, was the fundamental policy for the buildup of defense capability from 1977 to 1995. The second and current outline was created in 1995 to meet Japan's changing defense needs in the post–Cold War world. The

new outline addresses security requirements concerning regional conflicts and also covers the use of the Self-Defense Forces in disaster
relief and international peacekeeping operations. The objectives of the
new outline include streamlining Japan's defense capability to make it
more effective and efficient.

■Diplomacy

In a world environment marked by economic globalization and
ever-increasing interdependence in the international community,
Japan's security is integrally linked to, and dependent on, the peace
and stability of both the Asia-Pacific region and the rest of the world.
In order to ensure its own security as well as regional peace and stability, Japan is engaging in diplomacy at a number of levels. These efforts
include: (1) attempts to resolve individual conflicts and confrontations,
and bilateral and multilateral dialogues and cooperation to promote
regional stability; (2) political and security-related dialogues and cooperation, such as the ASEAN Regional Forum (ARF), aimed at increasing the policy transparency of Asia-Pacific countries and building trust
between them; and (3) the achievement of greater political stability in
the region through support for, and cooperation in, regional economic
development. In addition to the above, the Japanese government also
believes it is important to actively support arms control and disarma-
ment efforts and to participate in conflict prevention and peacekeeping
operations.

Growth

The first Shinkansen high-speed passenger railroad line began service
between Tokyo and Osaka on 1 October 1964, 9 days before the start of the Tokyo
Olympics. Greatly reducing travel times between Japan's principle
commercial cities, the Shinkansen system made a significant contribution
to the country's economic growth in the following decades. Traveling at speeds of
270 kilometers per hour on some routes, Shinkansen lines now run almost
the full length of Honshu and, via tunnel, to the island of Kyushu in the south.

Economy

Fortune

The *manekineko*, whose name translates literally as "beckoning cat," is a figurine of a sitting cat with its paw upraised in the Japanese gesture used to beckon someone. Occasionally still seen displayed at the front of shops, restaurants, and other businesses, the *manekineko* is thought to beckon good fortune and prosperity in through the door.

Contemporary Economy

The Japanese economy is the world's second largest market economy, behind the United States. Japan's real gross domestic product (GDP) was ¥535.7 trillion in fiscal 2000, and its per capita GDP ranked third among the 29 OECD countries in 1999. After more than three decades characterized primarily by solid growth, Japan's economy in the 1990s entered its most severe recession since World War II. The extended stagnation of the economy is evidence of problems in the structure of Japan's 50-year-old postwar economic system. The standardized mass production practices refined by Japanese industry have enabled Japan to produce automobiles, electronics, and many other products that are highly competitive internationally. However, as the world's economic focus shifts to software, information, and diversification, Japan needs to respond to changing economic trends. In order to promote economic recovery and facilitate growth in the 21st century, the government is reforming administrative operations, deregulating the economy, and liberalizing the financial system. The current difficult economic environment has already seen many bankruptcies and mergers among major financial institutions. Large manufacturing companies are also restructuring and forming alliances.

■High-Growth Era

At the end of the Allied Occupation in 1952, Japan ranked as a less-developed country, with per capita consumption a mere one-fifth that of the United States. During the period 1953–1973, the economy grew with

Per Capita GDP Ranking (1999)
(U.S. dollars)

1	Luxembourg	44,884	6	Denmark	32,763
2	Switzerland	36,339	7	Iceland	31,429
3	Japan	35,715	8	Sweden	26,941
4	Norway	34,360	9	Germany	25,728
5	United States	33,654	10	Austria	25,452

Source: Economic Planning Agency (now part of the Cabinet Office).

unprecedented rapidity (the average growth rate was 8.0% per annum overall and 10.6% during the 1960s). Real output per person in 1970 was 2.5 times higher than in 1960, and in 1968 Japan became the world's second largest economy. This rapid growth resulted in significant changes to Japan's industrial structure. Production shifted from a heavy reliance on agriculture and light manufacturing to a focus on heavy industry and, increasingly, services. Urbanization also progressed rapidly.

The first major expansion, the Iwato Boom (1959–1961, average growth 12.2%), touched off an investment spree, and growth reached 14.5 percent in 1961. Further expansions occurred in 1963–1964 (average growth 11.8%), 1966–1970 (the Izanagi Boom, average growth 11.6%), and 1972–1973 (the Tanaka expansion, average growth 8.9%).

Many factors contributed to rapid growth, including the shift in employment from low-productivity primary sector pursuits to manufacturing and a skilled and educated labor force with a strong commitment to work. In addition, macroeconomic policies were conducive to growth, the international environment was blessed with stable commodity prices and expanding trade, and investment was high. Together with the introduction of better technology, productivity increased rapidly.

Japan became a member of the International Monetary Fund (IMF) in 1952 and the General Agreement on Tariffs and Trade (GATT) in 1955. Around 1960, Japan committed itself to trade liberalization by seeking IMF article 8 status and deciding to join the OECD, both of which were realized in 1964. Tariffs and quantitative controls on most goods were removed by 1970, and, with the exception of agriculture and some high-technology products, most nontariff barriers were eliminated by the 1980s.

Indirect government assistance came in the form of tax breaks, treasury investment and loans, and the policy of administrative guidance of the Ministry of International Trade and Industry (now the Ministry of Economy, Trade and Industry). Most industries obtained some government favors, and it is unclear that any industry was effectively promoted relative to its rivals. However, domestic policies did result in a minimal presence by foreign firms in most sectors.

From the 1950s the banking system was gradually rebuilt. The stock exchange was reopened in 1949, but it did not develop into a major source of new funds until the 1980s. Corporate finance depended on bank financing as the major source of outside funds, giving rise to a capital structure dominated by debt. To prevent takeovers, enterprise groups, or *keiretsu*, actively sought cross-shareholdings with a variety of firms, including major financial institutions. Small and medium-sized enterprises remained relatively important during this period, employing nearly three-quarters of the labor force.

During the 1950s the major exporters—and thus the leading firms—were in textiles and other light industries, whose products were marketed by general trading companies; government promotion, however, focused on heavy manufacturing located in major coastal industrial complexes. During the 1960s the iron and steel industry and the shipbuilding industry came to the fore, followed by the chemical industry and in the early 1970s the electronics industry; the automotive industry rose to prominence in the late 1970s. Exports were important, espe-

©Kyodo

The opening ceremonies of the 18th Summer Olympic Games, held in Tokyo in October 1964. For many people, the hosting of this event represented Japan's return to international society after the long period of reconstruction following World War II.

cially for textiles and shipbuilding, which were aided by a rapid increase in world trade throughout the 1960s.

Rapid growth was not without its problems. Until the late 1960s, Japan faced chronic balance-of-payments difficulties. Inflation also proved to be problematic, at least comparatively. The spread of pollution and pollution-related diseases went unchecked until the late 1960s, when multiple fatalities from mercury and cadmium poisoning prompted more stringent pollution control laws.

■Mature Economy

By 1973, many of the factors that supported rapid growth lost their strength. First, Japanese industry had caught up with the best practices abroad; improving productivity required more resources than in the past. This in turn reduced the profitability of new investment, which fell to a lower level after 1974. The international environment also became less favorable, due mainly to the revaluation of the yen and trade friction with the United States. The Japan–United States textile talks of 1969, a worldwide commodity price boom that culminated in the quadrupling of oil prices during the oil crisis of 1973, and the movement of the yen to a floating rate in 1973 all worked to slow growth.

Even before the October 1973 oil crisis, the government had started to slow the economy in response to rising inflation. Combined with the impact of a quadrupling of oil prices, gross national product (GNP) fell 1.4 percent in 1974, the first actual decline since the 1950s. Growth slowed from the 10 percent level to an average of 3.6 percent during 1974–1979.

After the 1985 Plaza Accord, the yen rose sharply in value, reaching ¥120 to the U.S. dollar in 1988, twice its average 1984 value and three times its 1971 value. As a result, after 1986 the trade surplus gradually shrank. But this time around, domestic demand increased to pick up the slack. Monetary policy was eased four times during 1986, as the Bank of Japan lowered the discount rate from 5.0 percent to 2.5 percent, the lowest level since World War II. Consumption began increasing in 1986, and investment took over during 1987–1990; in fact, corporate investment rose to 19.6 percent of GNP in 1988 and 21.7 percent in 1989, exceeding total investment in plant and equipment in 1989 for the entire United States in both percentage and value.

With higher stock prices, new equity issues skyrocketed, becoming a significant source of finance for corporations for the first time since the crash of the Tokyo market in 1961. Banks found a new outlet for funds in real estate development. In turn, corporations attempted to maximize the productivity of their assets using real estate holdings as collateral for stock market speculation. The ensuing speculative binge (1986–1989) resulted in the so-called "bubble economy" in which land prices doubled and the Tokyo Nikkei stock market index rose 2.7 times.

Japan tightened monetary policy beginning in May 1989, and higher interest rates touched off a collapse of stock prices. By 1993 land prices in Tokyo had fallen 49.3 percent from the 1990 speculative peak, leaving major Japanese banks saddled with a large volume of bad debt.

According to the Economic Planning Agency (now part of the Cabinet Office), the Heisei Recession began in April 1991 and bottomed out in October 1993. The economic recovery since then, however, has been extremely slow. Subsequent upward momentum was undermined by negative factors such as the Asian economic crisis and the bankruptcy of several large financial institutions, and the Japanese economy turned downward again in 1997, suffering a negative growth rate of –1.1 percent in 1998. Aided by emergency government spending measures, increasing IT-product demand, and external demand growth caused by the economic recovery in Asia and a strong U.S. economy, Japan in 1999 showed some signs of recovery and achieved a small positive growth rate of 0.8 percent. At the beginning of the 21st century, however, the economy of Japan's key export market, the United States, appeared to be slowing and individual consumption—which represents 60 percent of domestic demand—continued to stagnate in Japan so there was considerable anxiety over near-term economic prospects.

Budget and Taxes

■Budget

The accounts of the national government are divided into the general account and special accounts, with the former regarded as the most important element of the Japanese fiscal system. Thus the term "budget" usually refers to the general account budget. Japan's fiscal year runs from April 1 through March 31.

National tax revenue belongs to the general account, with the exception of a small portion of tax revenues that belongs directly to special accounts. Tax and stamp revenues constitute approximately 60 percent of the total revenue. Until the early 1970s, public bond policy was restricted to construction bonds. Since 1975, however, huge bond

Composition of the General Account Budget (FY 2001)

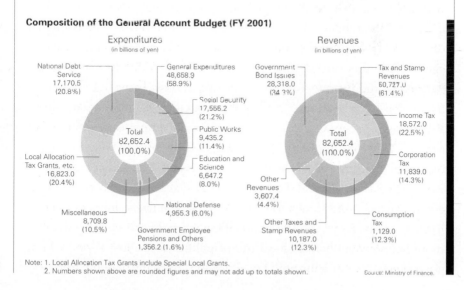

Expenditures
(in billions of yen)

Revenues
(in billions of yen)

National Debt Service 17,170.5 (20.8%)

General Expenditures 48,658.9 (58.9%)

Social Security 17,555.2 (21.2%)

Public Works 9,435.2 (11.4%)

Total 82,652.4 (100.0%)

Local Allocation Tax Grants, etc. 16,823.0 (20.4%)

Education and Science 6,647.2 (8.0%)

Miscellaneous 8,709.8 (10.5%)

National Defense 4,955.3 (6.0%)

Government Employee Pensions and Others 1,356.2 (1.6%)

Government Bond Issues 28,318.0 (34.3%)

Tax and Stamp Revenues 50,727.0 (61.4%)

Income Tax 18,572.0 (22.5%)

Total 82,652.4 (100.0%)

Corporation Tax 11,839.0 (14.3%)

Other Revenues 3,607.4 (4.4%)

Consumption Tax 1,129.0 (12.3%)

Other Taxes and Stamp Revenues 10,187.0 (12.3%)

Note: 1. Local Allocation Tax Grants include Special Local Grants.
2. Numbers shown above are rounded figures and may not add up to totals shown.

Source: Ministry of Finance.

issues (deficit-financing bonds) have been necessary to meet the budget deficit. Other revenue is composed of profits from government enterprises, receipts from the sale of government properties, miscellaneous receipts, and the carried-over surplus.

The special accounts are established by law when the government carries out specific projects or when it becomes necessary to administer revenue and expenditures separately from the general revenue and expenditures. In FY 2000 there were 38 special accounts, each with its own specific revenue sources, such as transfers from the general account, receipts from enterprises administered under the special accounts, and social insurance contributions. The revenue of some special accounts includes borrowing.

The budgets of government-affiliated corporations must be approved by the Diet. As part of the government's structural reforms, efforts are now under way to privatize or eliminate many such corporations.

■Taxes

The major emphasis of the Japanese tax system is on direct taxation, with approximately 60 percent of total tax revenue coming from direct taxes and the remaining 40 percent from indirect taxes. The principal direct tax is the national income tax, which can be classified into two categories. The first category being the progressive individual income tax defined in the Income Tax Law, and the second being the corporate income tax defined in the Corporation Tax Law. A 3-percent consumption tax was introduced in 1989, with the rate being raised to 5 percent in 1997. This consumption tax has increased the overall weight of indirect taxes in recent years. The general framework for local tax matters is established by the Local Tax Law. Local taxes include a prefectural enterprise tax, prefectural and municipal resident taxes, and a municipal fixed asset tax. However, the national government collects considerably more tax revenue than do local municipalities so it must support local government activities through tax allocations from the national treasury.

Fiscal Structural Reform

In the 1990s economic stagnation in Japan resulted in a worsening of the government's fiscal balance and a growing reliance on government debt. To deal with this increasing debt, in January 1997 the Conference on Fiscal Structural Reform was established. The Fiscal Structural Reform Act passed by the Diet in November 1997 called for the reduction of total national and local government debt to within 3 percent of the gross domestic product (GDP) by the year 2003, the elimination of new issues of deficit-financing bonds by the same year, and the holding of social security expenditure growth to no more than 2 percent in the years after fiscal 1999.

In 1998, however, there was a growing sense of urgency inside and outside the government over the need for strong action to stimulate the depressed economy and assist financial institutions struggling under a massive load of bad debt. As a result, implementation of the Fiscal Structural Reform Act was put on hold in December 1998, and the government instead reduced taxes and made large-scale public works investments in an attempt to stimulate the economy. This greatly worsened the government's fiscal balance, giving Japan the largest budget deficit and debt balance of any OECD nation. While taking measures for economic recovery, the government plans to check the worsening of the budget deficit by increasing the efficiency of government operations and promoting public sector reform of the central government, local governments, and the social security system.

Deregulation

The Japanese government is engaging in the drastic reform of Japan's economy and society in order to create a free and fair socioeconomic system that is fully opened to the international community and based on market principles and the concept of self-responsibility.

The overall trend in Japan since the 1950s has been toward gradual deregulation, often as a result of pressure from Japan's trading partners. Quotas and tariffs on manufactured and other goods were lowered progressively, especially as domestic industries became internationally competitive. As the country entered the 1980s, however, there was still extensive government regulation of private sector activities in areas such as banking, securities, foreign trade, foreign exchange, telecommunications, transportation, construction, land use, and pharmaceuticals.

The acceleration of deregulation activity in the 1980s resulted in three major public corporations being privatized to create Japan Tobacco, Inc., and Nippon Telegraph and Telephone Corporation (NTT) in 1985 and the Japan Railways (JR) group in 1987. The deregulation trend picked up further momentum in the 1990s. Specific examples include the loosening of restrictions on the communications, broadcasting, and distribution industries, but the most extensive deregulation took place in the financial markets with a series of reforms labeled the "Japanese Big Bang." These reforms included the liberalization of foreign exchange controls, the easing of restrictions on new financial instruments, and the elimination of regulations preventing banks, securities companies, and insurance companies from entering each other's markets.

Major government initiatives on deregulation in the past decade include the Plan to Promote Deregulation (1995), the Three-Year Program for Promoting Deregulation (1998), and the New Three-Year Program for Promoting Deregulation (2001).

National Income

Japan's national income in FY 1999 was ¥383 trillion. As a result of the economic slowdown, national income fell in FY 1999 for the second consecutive year, with the FY 1998 drop being the first recorded since this statistic began to be calculated in 1955.

As a general trend in national income distribution, over the past several decades the proportion of employee compensation has increased, whereas that of income from private corporations and private unincorporated entrepreneurial income has decreased. In FY 1970, employee compensation stood at 54.6 percent, while entrepreneurial income (private unincorporated and incorporated) was 37.1 percent. In FY 1999, these figures were 72.5 percent and 23.4 percent, respectively.

When expenditures, or disposition of national income, are broken down into consumption and savings, the share of savings in national disposable income steadily increased from about 20 percent in the 1950s, peaking at 31.1 percent in 1970. It then fell to an average of 17.3 percent in the 1994–1998 period. Even now, however, this figure is higher than that of other advanced nations.

Balance of Payments

The balance of payments is a statistical record of all economic transactions between residents of the reporting country and residents of all other countries. It is divided into the current account balance (which includes the balance on goods and services, the balance on income, and current transfers) and the capital balance.

Japan's current account balance fluctuated between deficit and surplus from the mid-1950s to the mid-1960s, reflecting the business cycle and the status of Japan's merchandise trade. Because of Japan's consistent merchandise trade surplus since that time, the current account balance has also consistently recorded a surplus, except for a few years of deficit caused by the two oil crises in the 1970s. The record high trade surplus of ¥14.0 trillion in 1998 resulted in a record high current account balance surplus of ¥15.8 trillion.

Data on Japan's balance on services since 1961 show a consistent trend toward larger and larger deficits because of Japan's deficits with respect to transport payments, tourism, and licensing fees. Another factor pushing up the services deficit since the mid-1980s has been the rise in the value of the yen.

The capital balance, which includes direct investment and portfolio investment transactions, has consistently recorded a deficit. The importance of the capital balance as a component of the international balance of payments has increased in the last decade, partly due to the large volume of capital movement that has accompanied global corporate restructuring activities.

Foreign Trade and Investment

Accelerating economic globalization continues to broaden and deepen Japan's trading and investment relationships with the countries of North America, Asia, and Europe. Centering its efforts on the World Trade Organization (WTO), Japan is working to promote multilateral trade and investment liberalization and the creation of international trade and investment rules.

■Trade

Immediately following World War II, the devastation of Japan caused a continuing foreign trade deficit as well as a chronic lack of foreign currency. It was not until the high-growth period of the late 1950s and early 1960s that export power increased significantly because of dramatic advances in manufacturing capacity and technology. Japan's trade balance began to show a surplus starting in the second half of the 1960s, although oil crises in 1973 and 1979 caused a temporary balance-of-trade deficit. Japan's trade surplus grew rapidly between the early 1980s and the early 1990s. After falling back somewhat in the mid-1990s, the surplus rose to an all-time high of ¥14.0 trillion in 1998 before retreating slightly to ¥12.3 trillion in 1999. Export levels fell in both 1998 and 1999, but there was also a slump in imports due to the economic stagnation in Japan. More than 50 percent of the 1999 trade surplus was with the United States.

Exports: In the 1950s and 1960s, the makeup of Japan's exports shifted to heavy-industry products and away from textiles and light-industry products. In the 1970s, the importance of industrial raw materials exports such as chemicals and steel dropped, and exports of machinery and electronics jumped as increasing emphasis was placed on high-value-added products. In the 1980s and 1990s, exports of technology-intensive products such as automobiles, computers, semiconductors, and machine tools continued to increase. Many Japanese companies, the most conspicuous being the automobile manufacturers, established local production facilities in the United States and Europe, partly in order to reduce trade friction. In an effort to maintain price competitiveness after the sharp rise in the value of the yen which began in 1985, many Japanese companies also moved the manufacturing of labor-intensive and technically less-complex parts and products to China and other Asian countries. In the 1980s, North America was the number one regional destination for Japanese exports, but in the 1990s the top spot was taken by Southeast Asia.

Imports: In the period immediately following World War II, raw fuels and textile raw materials made up the bulk of the imports. The relative importance of textile raw material imports decreased and that of mineral fuel and metal raw materials increased along with the development of Japanese heavy industry. As a result of the 1973 and 1979 oil crises, crude oil prices soared, and in 1980 mineral fuels were approximately 50 percent of total imports. By 1999 mineral fuels had fallen to 16.0 percent of imports.

The share of manufactured goods as a percentage of all Japanese imports has increased greatly since the mid-1980s, exceeding 50 percent in 1990 and reaching 62.4 percent in 1999. Part of the increase has been due to large-volume imports from the production facilities that Japanese companies established abroad, mainly in Asia, in response to the rising value of the yen. Food product imports are also increasing as a result of import liberalization of agricultural products.

■Investment

Direct overseas investment by Japanese companies rose rapidly in the second half of the 1980s as manufacturers shifted production facilities overseas in response to trade friction and the rise in the value of the yen. The investment level, which peaked in 1989, fluctuated in the 1990s before reaching a decade high of ¥7.4 trillion in 1999. The regional breakdown of this amount was Europe, 38.7 percent; North America, 37.1 percent; Central and South America, 11.2 percent; and Asia, 10.7 percent.

After falling somewhat in the mid-1990s, foreign direct investment in Japan grew dramatically between 1997 and 1999, when it reached an all-time high of ¥2.4 trillion. Major factors behind this sharp rise include the large increase in merger and acquisition activity by foreign companies in Japan and the growing number of Japanese companies—especially in the automobile, financial, and communications industries—which are actively seeking foreign investment. The extensive deregulation and legal and accounting system revisions that have taken place in Japan since the late 1980s have greatly facilitated the recent increase in foreign direct investment activity, which is being spurred on by growing economic globalization and the widespread view that international alliances will be an indispensable part of corporate strategy in the 21st century.

Industrial Structure

The industrial structure of a country is divided into three sectors: primary industries (agriculture, forestry, and fisheries), secondary industries (mining, manufacturing, and construction), and tertiary industries (power and water utilities, transportation, communications, retail and wholesale trade, banking, finance, real estate, business and personal services, and public administration).

From the 1950s through the 1980s economic growth in Japan was powered by industries manufacturing such products as iron and steel, ships, automobiles, and electrical goods. After the drastic rise in the value of the yen that began in 1985, however, industries such as shipbuilding contracted greatly due to a loss of international competitiveness, and companies producing automobiles, electrical goods, and many other products were forced to shift production overseas. Beginning in the 1990s, technological innovation in the electronics and information communications fields led to the expansion of information system use in many industries (finance, distribution, etc.) and to the development of information itself as a commodity. The resulting "service revolution" has significantly changed Japan's industrial structure, further increasing the weight of the tertiary sector as a percentage of the gross domestic product (GDP) and reducing the weight of the secondary sector.

In March 2000 the Industrial Structure Council of the Ministry of International Trade and Industry (now the Ministry of Economy, Trade and Industry) presented its final report concerning Japan's economic and industrial policy for the first quarter of the 21st century. This report touched on the need to decrease the size of government and utilize information technology to remodel the industrial structure. As fruitful areas for future development, the report also focused on "third-ware" industries fusing hardware and software, frontier industries such as aerospace, and industries that will help society deal with population aging and environmental problems.

The most recent stage in the development of national economies has been called postindustrialism, which is marked by a decrease in the employment share of the secondary sector and a shift from production of goods to services. This "service revolution" brings the continuing growth of tertiary industries; it seems to have begun in Japan in the mid-1970s, when manufacturing employment started to decline. In 1998 the tertiary sector accounted for 69.4 percent of total output and employed 62.7 percent, including public services, of the national labor force.

Employment

The employment system considered the norm in Japan from World War II up until recently was based on three essential institutions: lifetime employment, the seniority system, and enterprise unionism. Under lifetime employment companies recruit workers immediately upon graduation from a school or university, and these workers continue in the same company until retirement. Today lifetime employment practices are mostly limited to large firms and the public sector.

A busy crosswalk
at lunch time in
a Tokyo business district.

Under the seniority system an employee's rank, salary, and qualifications within a firm are based primarily on the length of service in the company. Under enterprise unionism union members bargain with management at the level of the individual enterprise.

With population aging, economic stagnation, business globalization, and other trends forcing structural changes in the labor market, it has become increasingly difficult for Japanese companies to maintain the traditional employment practices described above. Standardized raises based on length of service are giving way to performance-based raises at a rapidly growing number of large companies. While the custom of long-term employment at a single company remains deeply rooted in Japanese society, hiring practices are diversifying, and more companies are recruiting experienced people throughout the year as needed rather than simply hiring new graduates en masse on April 1st.

Another important factor in the transformation taking place in the labor market is the change in attitudes among the people being hired. The job turnover rate among young people is increasing as they become increasingly willing to change companies in search of more money, more job satisfaction, etc. The use of short-term employment contracts is increasing, and the ratio of part-time workers as a percentage of the total working population went from 15 percent in 1990 to 21 percent in 1998. Women represent approximately 70 percent of all part-time workers. Company use of temporary "dispatched" workers is increasing rapidly now that deregulation has made it possible for such people to be utilized in almost all types of jobs.

As a result of mismatches between supply and demand in the labor market and the bankruptcies and restructuring brought on by the economic recession, unemployment is at a high level for Japan. The unemployment rate, which had been below 2 percent in the 1960s and 1970s, rose rapidly after 1993, reaching 5.5 percent in November 2001. The difficult employment environment is expected to continue.

Energy Sources

Japan's energy options are seriously limited by its lack of domestic energy sources coupled with the huge energy demands of its industries. Japan's dependence on imports for its primary energy supply was 43.4 percent in 1960 and 80 percent in 1998.

Although Japan remains heavily dependent on imported oil, as a result of conservation efforts and development of other energy sources oil's share of the country's total energy supply dropped from 73.4 percent in 1975 to 52.4 percent in 1998. During the same period nuclear power jumped from 1.5 to 13.7 percent and natural gas went from 2.5 to 12.3 percent while coal stayed at 16.4 percent and hydroelectric power dropped from 5.3 to 3.9 percent.

The above changes reflect the electric power industry's efforts, following the 1973 oil shock, to reduce its reliance on oil by switching to other thermal sources (natural gas and coal) and to nuclear power. In 1999 total electric power generated amounted to 1,066 billion kilowatt hours, of which thermal power plants (oil, liquid natural gas, and coal) supplied 61 percent; nuclear power plants, 30 percent; and hydroelectric power plants and alternative energy sources, 9 percent.

Taking into account air pollution and other environmental issues and the limited number of resource alternatives available for large-scale power generation, nuclear energy cannot help playing an important role as a substitute for oil and as an energy source that does not produce CO_2. As of June 2000 Japan had 52 nuclear power plants in operation with a total power generation capacity of 45.08 million kilowatts. Although construction of additional nuclear power plants is planned, the series of nuclear-power-related accidents that have occurred in recent years have greatly shaken the public's confidence in the safety of nuclear energy.

Energy conservation constitutes one of the pillars of Japan's energy policy and many efforts are being made to increase efficiency in energy use. However, great conservation efforts have already been made in industry, and most industries will find it extremely difficult to raise efficiency further. Per capita energy consumption in Japan in 1997 was at the relatively low level of about 4.08 metric tons oil equivalent, as against 8.10 metric tons oil equivalent in the United States.

As part of the New Sunshine Project, which began in 1993, Japan is working to develop new energy sources, energy conservation methods, and technologies to safeguard the global environment. If this project succeeds in its goals, by 2030 Japan will be getting one-third of its energy from new sources and will have cut its CO_2 emissions by 50 percent.

Science and Technology

As it enters the 21st century, Japanese science and technology has, in general, moved beyond the "catch up" era that characterized much of the last century. With regard to basic research and development and the R&D environment, however, there are still areas where Japan lags behind the United States and Europe. In 1995 the government passed the Science and Technology Basic Law as the backbone of its policy to promote science and technology as a critical national issue for insuring that Japan is a front-runner in the new century. This law requires the government to prepare Science and Technology Basic Plans setting forth in detail its policy for the promotion of science and technology. The first plan, which covered the period from 1996 to 2000, specified an overall five-year science and technology budget scale of ¥17 trillion and recommended the construction of a new R&D system to facilitate creative R&D activities. The second plan, for 2001 to 2005, focuses on the reform of science and technology systems and the prioritized promotion of research. Strategic investments are to be made in the following four priority areas: bioscience, information communications, the environment, and nanotechnology/materials. The budget defined in the second plan is ¥24 trillion.

R&D Funding: Japan's R&D expenditures in the natural sciences in fiscal 1998 were ¥14.8 trillion, which was 3 percent of the GDP. Although the government provided only about 20 percent of these funds, with the remaining 80 percent coming from the private sector, government investment in science and technology has been increasing steadily since the enactment of the Science and Technology Basic Law. Of the total expenditures, 61.4 percent was used for development, 24.6 percent for applied research, and 13.9 percent for basic research.

R&D Personnel: As of April 1999 there were 639,000 researchers active in Japan, with 67.2 percent working in corporations, 26.1 percent in universities, and 6.7 percent in research institutions.

Technology Trade: The technology trade balance is one indicator of a country's R&D and technology capabilities. In fiscal 1998 Japan recorded its sixth consecutive technology-trade surplus at ¥486 billion, with receipts exceeding payments by a factor of 2.13. By far the greatest surplus was in the transportation equipment field.

■**International Cooperation in Science and Technology**

Japan is promoting information exchange, personnel exchange, and joint research activities in a variety of fields, including nuclear energy, space technology, marine science, life sciences, and environmental protection.

Bilateral Cooperation: Japan has concluded bilateral agreements on cooperation in science and technology R&D with around 30 countries and agreements on cooperation in developing peaceful uses of nuclear energy with 6 countries. It has also concluded bilateral agreements covering fields such as environmental protection and space development with a number of countries.

Incorporating sophisticated electronics technology, the Aibo robot dog was a big hit when it was introduced by Sony in 1999.

©Sony Corporation

Multilateral Cooperation: Japan provides funding and personnel for the operations of various international organizations, such as the International Atomic Energy Agency and the committees of the Economic and Social Council of the United Nations. The Human Frontier Science Program, which was proposed by Japan in 1987, has in the past 10 years provided over 400 grants for research in the neurosciences. Participating countries include Japan, the United States, Canada, and many European countries. As part of the International Space Station project, Japan is providing the experiment module *Kibo.*

■Nuclear Power Development and Use

The development and use of nuclear power in Japan is carried out in accordance with the Long-Term Program for Research, Development and Utilization of Nuclear Energy, a plan prepared every five years (most recently in November 2000) by the Atomic Energy Commission. Nuclear power plants currently provide approximately one-third of Japan's electricity. The Japan Nuclear Cycle Development Institute and the Japan Atomic Energy Research Institute are the principal organizations involved in developing nuclear-energy-related technology. Areas in which R&D is currently taking place include reprocessing of spent fuel, development of fast breeder reactors, and disposal of high-level radioactive waste.

■Space Technology

Japan's space research program is proceeding in line with the Fundamental Policy of Space Activities, which was last revised in 1996.

Space technology development is coordinated by two organizations: the National Space Development Agency of Japan (NASDA) and the Institute of Space and Astronautical Science (ISAS).

When its first successful experimental satellite, *Osumi*, was launched in 1970, Japan became the fourth country to achieve satellite launch capability, following the Soviet Union, the United States, and France. As of December 1999 Japan's total satellite launches numbered 81.

The development of the first of the H series of rockets, the H-I, was completed in 1986 in response to the need for launch vehicles for heavy applications satellites. The H-I, a three-stage rocket 40 meters in length and weighing 140 metric tons, was capable of placing a 550-kilogram satellite into geostationary orbit. The two-stage liquid-propellant H-II rocket was based entirely on domestic technology. First launched in 1994, it is 49 meters long and weighs 260 metric tons. Development work continues on the H-IIA, which is designed to meet the diversifying launch demands of the 21st century with low cost and a high degree of reliability. The H-IIA launch vehicle family consists of a standard vehicle and an augmented vehicle, with the latter being able to launch a seven-ton-class payload into geostationary orbit as a result of the addition of a large liquid rocket booster to the standard vehicle.

©NASDA

The H-IIA is shown here making a successful launch on 29 August 2001.

■Life Sciences

Research and development in the life sciences in Japan is being promoted by the government under the Basic Plan for Research and Development on the Life Sciences, which was prepared in 1997. According to this plan, the fields that should be given particular attention by the government are: R&D on living organisms as integrated systems (including research on brain function, cancer mechanisms, and the functions of individual plants and animals in the ecosystem and biosphere) and R&D on basic biological molecules (including genome research). The plan also considers the bioethics issues presented by new techniques such as cloning.

Japanese life science research in areas such as the sequencing of the rice genome and the clarification of the structure of proteins is currently generating interest around the world. In one of the most important scientific frontiers remaining in the 21st century, Japanese brain science researchers are working to understand how the brain works, protect the brain from disease and malfunction, and develop computers that simulate brain functions.

■Marine Science and Technology

Japanese government policy on ocean development is formulated by the Council for Ocean Development. A wide range of marine research is being carried out using the state-of-the-art equipment of the Japan Marine Science and Technology Center. The oceanographic research vessel *Mirai* is being used to investigate the ocean's ecosystem and thermal cycle and the dynamics of the seafloor. Deep sea research is being carried out using the manned research submersibles *Shinkai 2000* and *Shinkai 6500* and the unmanned vehicles *Dolphin-3K* and *Kaiko*. The TRITON moored buoy network is being used to study surface meteorology and upper ocean conditions as part of international climate research programs.

Gathering

Neighborhood groups, known as *kumi*, were at one time
an important part of both village and city life in Japan.
Members of these groups together planted rice, prepared for festivals,
built and repaired homes and roads, and aided each other
in times of need. Although a mandatory system of
neighborhood groups no longer exists, growing emphasis is
being placed on the role of voluntary neighborhood associations
in building community ties and improving local life.

Society

祝

Shichigosan, which translates literally as "seven-five-three," is the custom of taking three- and five-year-old boys and three- and seven-year-old girls to a Shinto shrine in mid-November to pray for their safe and healthy future. For many children today, Shichigosan is their only chance to get all dressed up in traditional attire.

Social Security Programs

Japan's social security programs consist of social insurance, which includes health and medical insurance, long-term care insurance, public pensions, employment insurance, and workers' compensation; social welfare services for older people, children, and handicapped persons; public health programs for public sanitation, infectious disease treatment, etc.; and assistance for war victims. In FY 2000 social security-related expenses accounted for 19.7 percent of the general account expenditure of the national budget. In FY 1998 the volume of Japan's social security benefits was ¥69.4 trillion yen, which was 17.8 percent of national income. Per capita benefits were ¥550,000. Combined taxes and social insurance fees were 36.9 percent of national income in FY 2000.

■**Medical and Health Insurance**

The cornerstone of the present system of public health insurance is the 1922 Health Insurance Law, providing coverage primarily for factory workers and miners. By the enforcement in 1961 of an amended Health Insurance Law all Japanese citizens and aliens resident in Japan have been entitled to coverage under one of four alternative health insurance plans: employees' health insurance, which covers most private-sector employees; National Health Insurance; mutual aid associations for teachers and public-service employees; and Seamen's Insurance. By 1980, 99.3 percent of the total population was covered under one of the four plans; the remaining 0.7 percent was covered by

Taxes and Social Security Fees as a Percentage of National Income

(in percentages)

	Social security fees	Taxes	Total
Japan (FY2000)	14.4	22.5	36.9
United States (1997)	10.1	27.5	37.6
United Kingdom (1996)	10.2	38.7	48.9
Germany (1997)	26.7	29.2	55.9
France (1997)	28.3	36.3	64.6

Source: Ministry of Finance.

the medical assistance program. Under most Japanese medical insurance plans, members are required to pay 20 to 30 percent of their medical expenses, depending on the type of treatment provided; the insurance carrier then remunerates the doctor, hospital, clinic, or other medical care provider directly for the remainder on a fee-for-service basis as determined by the Ministry of Health, Labour and Welfare.

National Health Insurance covers the self-employed and their dependents, retired persons, and various other categories of individuals ineligible for employees' health insurance or any of the other medical and health insurance plans. In 1958 the New National Health Insurance Law gave the responsibility of overseeing the insurance to local governments. Under the present system premiums are paid solely by the insured. The amount of the premium varies from one municipality to another. The system also receives financial assistance from the national treasury.

■Long-Term Care Insurance

A long-term care insurance system was implemented in April 2000 to help care for the growing population of elderly. This system collects obligatory insurance contributions from all persons aged 40 or older and provides such services as home visits by home helpers and long-term stays in nursing homes. The financing comes from the national government (25%), local governments (25%), and insurance contributions (50%).

■Pensions

The Japanese pension system centers on the National Pension, which is administered by the national government. The National Pension provides basic, mandatory pension coverage, including old-age, disability, and survivor benefits, to all Japanese citizens. People aged 20 to 60 contribute to this pension and receive benefits beginning at age 65. As of March 1998, 70.3 million citizens were enrolled. In 2000 the monthly payment required of all individual contributors to the National Pension system was ¥13,300. The minimum contributory period to receive benefits is 25 years; the full benefit of ¥67,017 per month (as of April 2000) is received for 40 years of contributions. Two supplemental programs provide additional coverage and benefits. The Employees' Pension Insurance program provides coverage for 33.5 million private-sector employees. Mutual aid association pensions enroll an additional 5.3 million public employees and teachers. Seeking to improve the future financial viability of the public pension system, in 2000 the government enacted legislation to cut employee and mutual aid association pension benefits and gradually raise the age at which benefits start being received from 60 to 65.

Aging Population

The Japanese population is aging faster than any other in the world, a situation which is causing serious problems for society. The percentage of Japan's population aged 65 or over was only at the 7 percent level in 1970, but just 25 years later in 1995 it reached 14.6 percent. Average life expectancy went from 69.31 for men and 74.66 for women in 1970 to 77.10 for men and 83.99 for women in 1999, and during the same period the total fertility rate fell from 2.13 to 1.34. It has been projected that as a result of these trends by 2050 one in every three Japanese alive will be 65 or older.

Ratio of the Population Aged 65 and Older in Selected Countries
(in percentages)

	1975	1985	1995	2000	2010	2020	2030
Japan	7.9	10.3	14.6	17.4	22.0	26.9	28.0
United States	10.5	11.8	12.5	12.5	13.2	16.6	20.7
United Kingdom	14.0	15.1	15.9	16.0	17.1	19.8	23.1
Germany	14.8	14.6	15.5	16.4	19.8	21.6	26.2
France	13.5	13.0	15.0	16.0	16.7	20.2	23.2
Sweden	15.1	17.9	17.6	17.4	19.5	23.1	25.5

Note: Figures for 2000 and after are projections.
Source: National Institute of Population and Social Security Research.

Life Expectancy at Birth

	Male	Female
Japan (1999)	77.10	83.99
France (1998)	74.60	82.20
Sweden (1993–1997)	76.18	81.39
Germany (1994–1996)	73.29	79.72
United Kingdom (1996)	74.31	79.48
United States (1997)	73.60	79.40

Source: Ministry of Health, Labour and Welfare.

The aging population is placing an increasingly heavy burden on the medical care and pension systems, and in the years ahead a shrinking working population will have to shoulder the growing cost of this burden. The government is now attempting to restructure the social security system.

Life Cycle

The life cycle of the Japanese people has evolved over time and has been altered radically by the institutions of 20th-century mass society and by the greater longevity of modern populations. The following outline depicts life stages as a typical individual might pass through them.

■**Infancy**

One month after birth the infant may be taken to a local Shinto shrine to be introduced to the guardian gods and symbolically to all of society (*miyamairi*). Annual celebrations for children occur on 3 March for girls (Doll Festival), on 5 May for boys (Children's Day), and on 15 November for girls aged three and seven and boys aged three and five (Shichigosan).

■**Childhood (about 7–13 years)**

Under the modern school system in Japan the most important rites of passage are school enrollment and graduation. The nine years of compulsory education comprise six years of elementary school and three years of middle school. Children who turn six years old by 1 April each year are enrolled in elementary school, and start their school careers by participating in an enrollment ceremony.

■Youth (about 13–25 years)

More than 95 percent of Japanese young people complete high school, and almost half of them enter a university or college. Today one attains legal maturity at age 20, and municipal governments celebrate Coming-of-Age Day (Seijin no Hi) for 20-year-olds on the second Sunday in January.

■Maturity (about 26–60 years)

On average, both men and women marry around the ages 27 to 29. A man's life tends to be focused on his job although in recent years a growing number of fathers have been actively participating in child raising. Most women find paid work after leaving school and an increasing number are able to sustain long-term occupational careers. Women today generally give birth to only one to three children, and after their children are all in school many find jobs.

■Old Age (about 61 and over)

The 60th birthday, when the zodiac signs complete a full cycle (*kanreki*), was the traditional beginning of old age. Retirement usually occurs around age 60. Almost all Japanese are covered by the National Pension, which begins paying benefits at age 65, but the monthly payment is quite small. Long-term employees are also covered by Employees' Pension Insurance; the age at which benefit payments start under this program is being gradually raised from 60 to 65.

■After Death

About 90 percent of the funerals held in Japan use Buddhist rites. In Buddhist tradition, at death an individual is given a posthumous name by the priest of the family temple. In the early weeks and months after death, frequent rites are held to comfort the soul. Thereafter, deathday anniversaries are honored for up to 50 years.

Family

Prior to World War II the family was organized as a hierarchy with the male household head at the apex, theoretically in a position of absolute authority over others. After the war a Civil Code revision abolished this authority and established a legal basis for equality between men and women, husbands and wives, and parents and children.

The typical Japanese family today—a nuclear family with a mother, father, and one or two children—is a product of a number of interrelated postwar-period trends, such as the sharp reduction in the average number of children per family, the increase in life expectancy, and the concentration of the population in urban areas where small dwellings are the norm. As a result of Japan's postwar economic growth, almost all families consider themselves middle class and, in fact, the urban middle-class family is the dominant type and model for all Japan. Middle-class ideals and standards of living have penetrated rural areas as well.

Although multiunit dwellings have become the norm in large cities, most Japanese families aspire to own a single-family home. A 1998 study found that single-family-owned homes have an average of 6 rooms and 122.74 square meters of floor space. Most houses have both Japanese-style rooms with *tatami* mats and Western-style rooms with

Household Composition

(in percentages)

	1975	1980	1985	1990	1995	1998
Nuclear families	58.7	60.3	61.1	60.0	58.9	58.6
Married couples without dependents	11.8	13.1	14.6	16.6	18.4	19.7
Married couples with children	42.7	43.1	41.9	38.2	35.3	33.6
Single parents with children	4.2	4.2	4.6	5.1	5.2	5.3
Three-generation households	16.9	16.2	15.2	13.5	12.5	11.5
Single-person households	18.2	18.1	18.4	21.0	22.6	23.9
Other	6.2	5.4	5.3	5.6	6.1	6.0

(in thousands)

	1975	1980	1985	1990	1995	1998
Number of households	32,877	35,338	37,226	40,273	40,770	44,496

Source: Ministry of Health, Labour and Welfare.

carpeted or bare-wood floors.

According to 1998 census data, 58.6 percent of all households are nuclear families and 23.9 percent are single-person households. Compared to 1985, the percentage of single-person households is considerably higher, and the average family size, at 2.81, is down. An integral part of these trends is the rapid increase in the average age of the population. The number of persons aged 65 or over living alone is increasing rapidly as is the number of nuclear families that consist only of an elderly couple (husband 65 or over, wife 60 or over). The number of households with children (unmarried persons under age 18) continues to fall, and the average number of children in those households is down to 1.8. Approximately 50 percent of all households with children have 2 children.

Despite the changes taking place in society, the Japanese family is still characterized by stability and continuity. Although the number of women working after marriage is increasing, roles within the family are still clearly differentiated in most cases. The husband nominally heads the family and bears clear responsibility for financial support. However, he is likely to be focused primarily on his work, letting his wife take effective charge of the house and children. The number of divorces per 1,000 people went from 0.93 in 1970 to 1.94 in 1998. The overall percentage of people aged 65 and over who live with their children is falling, but the older an elderly person is the more likely he or

Tracks of developer-built houses are a common sight within commuting distance of major urban centers such as Tokyo, Osaka, and Nagoya.

she is to be living with a son or daughter. Over 70 percent of persons aged 85 or over are living with their children.

Women in Japan

Japanese history provides striking examples of how changes in the status of women can be linked with other broad socioeconomic trends. A woman-centered marriage pattern in ancient times contributed to considerable religious and political influence for women, but from the 6th century onward the growing acceptance of Confucian and Buddhist precepts that maintained women's inferiority reflected and reinforced a shift toward patriarchal family structure. Only since the Meiji period (1868–1912), and especially since World War II, have increasing educational and employment opportunities, as well as improvements in legal status, allowed women intellectual and financial autonomy once again.

The number of women who pursue higher education in Japan has increased every year since World War II. In fact, in 1989 the percentages of females entering universities and junior colleges exceeded that of males for the first time. About 50 percent of female high school gradu-

Women within the Total Population of Employed Persons

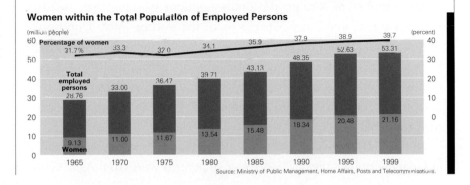

Source: Ministry of Public Management, Home Affairs, Posts and Telecommunications.

ates now go on to higher education, and more than half of these women enroll in four-year institutions, the rest opting for junior colleges.

The 1985 Equal Employment Opportunity Law for Men and Women stipulated that employers must make an effort to offer women equal opportunities for employment and promotion and that they are prohibited from dismissing women employees who require maternity leave. A revision to this law was passed in 1997; it explicitly prohibits gender discrimination in job advertisements, hiring, assignments, and promotions. A childcare leave system that was implemented in 1992 has begun to show some effect as the number of women who take advantage of it is gradually increasing; nevertheless, improving the working environment and childcare infrastructure for women who want to have children while continuing to work are two major issues that Japan has yet to satisfactorily address.

Japanese women gained full political rights in 1945, when the Election Law was revised to permit them to vote and to run for political office. Women also play a major role in the consumer movement and citizens' movements.

Foreigners in Japan

The number of foreign nationals resident in Japan has steadily increased and stood at 1,556,113 as of the end of 1999. This figure includes only foreigners registered in accordance with the Alien Registration Law. The largest national group, accounting for 40.9 percent of the total, is composed of Koreans, followed by citizens of China and Brazil. Some 50 percent of registered aliens in Japan are permanent residents.

Of the 45,000 foreign students with student visas who were enrolled at Japanese universities in 1999, over 90 percent were from Asia. China and the Republic of Korea together represented 75 percent of the total. The goal of the Ministry of Education, Culture, Sports, Science and Technology is to increase the number of foreign students to 100,000.

Environmental Quality

Environmental pollution in Japan has accompanied industrialization since the Meiji period (1868–1912). In the era of rapid growth following World War II, Japan became one of the most polluted countries in the world. The strict environmental protection measures that were subsequently implemented have reduced pollution caused by industrial drainage and air pollutant emissions. On the other hand, pollution from chemical substances such as asbestos and dioxin and problems with processing nuclear, industrial, and household wastes are becoming increasingly serious. Global environmental issues like the destruction of the ozone layer and global warming cannot be resolved by a single country, so it is clear that the cooperation of all countries is increasingly necessary to protect the environment. Japan plays an active role in this global effort. The Third Session of the Conference of the Parties to the United Nations Framework Convention on Climate Change (COP3) was held in Kyoto in December 1997.

■**Antipollution and Environmental Preservation Policies**

The Pollution Countermeasures Basic Law passed in 1967 sought to create common principles and policies for pollution control in all government agencies and to promote an integrated effort to clean up the environment. The Basic Law indicates the responsibilities of the central government, local governments, and business firms with regard to controlling pollution. In addition, the Basic Law laid the framework for establishing environmental quality standards, drafting pollution-control programs, and aiding victims of diseases caused by pollution.

The Pollution Countermeasures Basic Law, however, applies only to certain types of pollution, and so it has become increasingly difficult to address new global environmental problems using its provisions. For this reason, in 1993 the government enacted the Basic Environmental Law to facilitate implementation of comprehensive and systematic measures to protect the environment, and it is actively working to promote environmental preservation worldwide through international cooperation and a rethinking of high-volume consumption practices in society. In 1997 the Environmental Impact Assessment Law was enacted. This law defines requirements for assessment of the environmental impact of large-scale public- and private-sector projects.

In the 1990s pollution from dioxin released by trash incinerators became a major issue in society. Dioxin is known to cause cancer, and recent research has focused on the dangers of dioxin as a hormone disrupting chemical. The Law Concerning Special Measures Against Dioxin, which went into effect in 1999, includes provisions covering regulation of dioxin emission, monitoring of effects on health and the environment, and preparation of government plans for reducing emissions.

The amount of general (non-industrial) waste generated in Japan

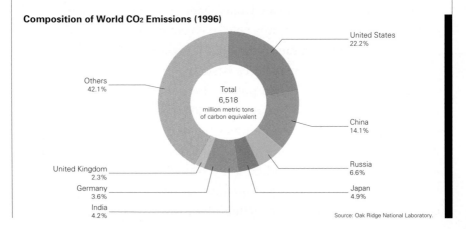

Composition of World CO_2 Emissions (1996)

United States 22.2%

Others 42.1%

Total 6,518 million metric tons of carbon equivalent

China 14.1%

United Kingdom 2.3%

Germany 3.6%

India 4.2%

Russia 6.6%

Japan 4.9%

Source: Oak Ridge National Laboratory.

Percentage of General Waste Recycled in Japan

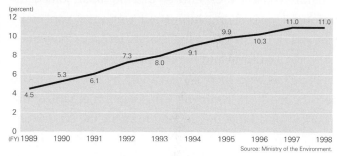

(percent)

(FY)	1989	1990	1991	1992	1993	1994	1995	1996	1997	1998
	4.5	5.3	6.1	7.3	8.0	9.1	9.9	10.3	11.0	11.0

Source: Ministry of the Environment.

has exceeded 50 million tons a year since 1990. This has increased the emphasis on recycling in Japan, which has one of the highest used paper recycling rates in the world. The implementation of the Receptacle Packaging Recycle Law in April 1997 placed the responsibility for recycling polyethylene terephthalate (PET) bottles, glass bottles, and paper and plastic packaging on the manufacturer.

Electrical products discarded by Japanese households have almost all been disposed of in landfills. The Specific Household Electrical Appliance Recycling Law, which went into effect in 2001, obligates manufacturers to recycle the materials from air conditioners, televisions, refrigerators, and washing machines.

In 2001 the Environment Agency, which had been created in 1971, was upgraded to cabinet ministry level, becoming the Ministry of the Environment.

■Conservation

In response to the sharp deterioration in the natural environment caused by the postwar period of rapid economic growth, the Nature Conservation Law was passed in 1972 to serve as the basis for all legal measures to protect the natural environment. To protect nature and promote recreation, an extensive system of national parks, quasi-national parks, and prefectural natural parks was established.

As part of its nature conservation efforts, in 1980 Japan joined the Ramsar Convention for preserving important wetlands, especially waterfowl habitats, and in 1992 it joined the World Heritage Convention for protecting the world's cultural and natural heritage.

In recent years there has been increasing activity by citizens' groups working to protect the local environment. Conservation organizations from across the country joined together in 1992 to create the Association of National Trust in Japan.

School System

The first modern school system in Japan was established by the Education Order of 1872. Modeled on school systems of Western Europe, the pre-World War II schools in Japan were controlled by the state. The Japanese school system has undergone substantial change since World War II. The Educational Reforms of 1947 decentralized control of education. The Fundamental Law of Education, which was enacted as part of these reforms, stated the basic aims of the educa-

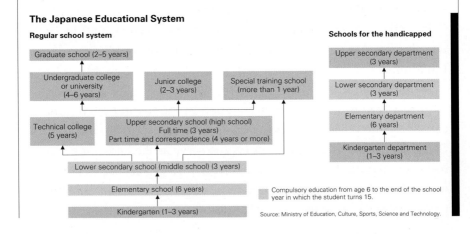

The Japanese Educational System

Regular school system — Schools for the handicapped

Graduate school (2–5 years)

Undergraduate college or university (4–6 years) — Junior college (2–3 years) — Special training school (more than 1 year)

Technical college (5 years) — Upper secondary school (high school) Full time (3 years) Part time and correspondence (4 years or more)

Lower secondary school (middle school) (3 years)

Elementary school (6 years)

Kindergarten (1–3 years)

Upper secondary department (3 years)

Lower secondary department (3 years)

Elementary department (6 years)

Kindergarten department (1–3 years)

Compulsory education from age 6 to the end of the school year in which the student turns 15.

Source: Ministry of Education, Culture, Sports, Science and Technology.

Left: Elementary school classroom.
Right: Lower secondary school (middle school) computer class.

tional system: contributing to the peace and welfare of humanity, the full development of personality, and the creation of love for truth and justice among students. The law also contained a commitment to academic freedom, equal opportunity, and coeducation.

The nucleus of the school system is the 6-3-3-4 system of six-year elementary schools, three-year middle schools, three-year high schools, and four-year universities. In addition there are kindergartens, five-year technical colleges for graduates of middle school, and schools for the handicapped. Universities include undergraduate colleges, junior colleges, and graduate schools. Aside from these regular schools there are vocational and technical training schools. Education is compulsory only through middle school, but high school education is nearly universal. In 1999 the percentage of Japanese students continuing their education at a junior college or university was 46.8 percent for men and 49.6 percent for women. The great majority of schools at all levels are coeducational. Over 95 percent of elementary and middle schools are public; private schools play a larger role at the secondary and university level (about 30 percent of Japan's high schools and about 80 percent of its universities and colleges are private institutions).

■**Educational Reforms**

A number of reforms affecting the entire Japanese educational system from elementary schools through universities are now under way. In 1997 and 1998 the Central Council for Education, which serves as a decision-making body for government education policy, issued reports on three subjects: education in the 21st century, education for the human heart from early childhood, and local educational administration. The recommendations in these reports have led to greater diversity in the educational system, with, for example, the establishment of combined middle and high schools and the implementation of procedures for permitting college admission after completion of only two years of high school.

■School Course Guidelines

The Ministry of Education, Culture, Sports, Science and Technology prepares guidelines containing basic outlines of each subject taught in Japanese schools and the objectives and content of teaching in each grade. First drawn up in 1947, these guidelines are revised every 10 years or so. The 1989 revisions stressed computer and foreign language literacy for the new age of information and internationalization. The 1998 revisions prepare for the change to a five-day school week that is to take effect throughout Japan in April 2002. The most important changes involve reductions in class time and course content.

■School System Administration

The Ministry of Education, Culture, Sports, Science and Technology

Advancing to University

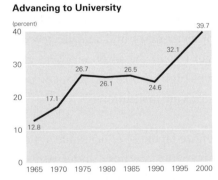

Advancing to Graduate School

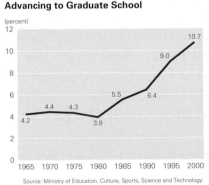

Source: Ministry of Education, Culture, Sports, Science and Technology.

handles all administrative affairs concerning education at the national level. Its jurisdiction includes establishment and administration of national schools, approval of the establishment of public and private universities, and authorization of school textbooks.

The local educational administrative body is the board of education. These boards exist at the prefectural and municipal levels. Board members are appointed by the head of the prefectural or municipal assembly. The boards have authority over the establishment and administration of public schools, curriculum management, the appointment of personnel, and the planning of study and training projects for teachers.

■School Textbooks

In Japan all elementary, middle, and high schools use government-authorized textbooks. Textbooks are compiled by private publishers, who are given a certain amount of freedom in the style of presentation, but are also required to conform to the stipulated courses of study. Authorization is given after screening of the textbooks by the Ministry of Education, Culture, Sports, Science and Technology.

A system of free distribution of textbooks for compulsory education was established in 1963. The textbooks used in each school district are chosen by the local board of education from among those authorized by the central government; in the case of private schools the responsibility lies with the school principal.

Transportation

Japan has a highly developed domestic and international transportation network. The system as it now exists was developed in the century following the Meiji Restoration of 1868, but even earlier the transportation system was relatively sophisticated for a preindustrial society.

Commuting at rush hour.

Calculated on a passenger-kilometer basis, passenger transportation shares in 1999 were: motor vehicles, 67.1 percent; railroads, 27.0 percent; airlines, 5.6 percent; and ships, 0.3 percent. In the same year, the breakdown for freight transportation, calculated on a ton-kilometer basis, was: motor vehicles, 54.8 percent; coastal shipping, 41.0 percent; railroads, 4.0 percent; and airlines, 0.2 percent. At present most of the components of Japan's transportation network are privately operated. Since the 1990s the government has proceeded with an active program of deregulation of the transportation field.

■Railroads

The core of Japan's network of railways is the JR (Japan Railways) group, which was created when the Japanese National Railways (JNR) was privatized in 1987. The JR group is made up of six passenger railway companies, a freight railway company, and several other affiliated companies. In 1998 the passenger rail system comprised 27,182 operation-kilometers, of which JR companies operated 20,059 or 74 percent of the total. JR passenger service includes intercity trunk lines, urban feeder services, and a large number of rural lines. It also operates Japan's fastest passenger trains on the Shinkansen (bullet train) lines. The JR group's Japan Freight Railway Co. provides almost all of the rail freight service in Japan.

In addition to the JR group companies, 16 large railway companies and more than 100 smaller railways provide regional transportation.

There were non-JR subway networks operating in Tokyo, Osaka, Nagoya, Kobe, Sapporo, Yokohama, Kyoto, Fukuoka, and Sendai as of 2000. More than 8 million passengers a day travel on the 12 Tokyo subway lines and approximately 2.6 million travel on the 7 Osaka subway lines. Subway lines are designed to connect directly with existing suburban surface rail networks.

■Shinkansen

A high-speed passenger railroad system consisting of five regular Shinkansen lines where the trains run only on special Shinkansen tracks, and two lines, usually referred to as "Mini-Shinkansen" lines, where the trains run both on Shinkansen tracks and standard local tracks. The addition of several other Shinkansen lines has been planned since 1973, and construction continues on some sections of those lines.

The Tokaido Shinkansen serves the 500-kilometer (311-mi) Tokyo-Osaka corridor that has long been considered the main artery of Japan. This line runs at a maximum speed of 270 kilometers per hour, and the minimum trip time between Tokyo and Osaka is now 2 hours 30 minutes. A Shinkansen train departs Tokyo for Osaka or some point further west about every six minutes throughout most daytime schedules. Since it was inaugurated in 1964, the Shinkansen has had a remarkable record of high-speed operation, safety, volume of transport, and punctuality.

■Motor Vehicles

In spite of urban traffic congestion and the high cost of fuel, private

©JR Tokai

New 700-series Shinkansen trains like this one travel between Tokyo and Hakata in Kyushu at speeds up to 270 kilometers per hour.

automobiles have been one of the fastest growing segments of passenger transportation. The number of registered motor vehicles increased from only about 3.4 million in 1960 to 75.9 million in December 2000, with 69.4 percent of the 2000 total being passenger cars. Japan operated a total of 7,843 kilometers of high-standard trunk roads and 616 kilometers of urban expressways in 2000.

■Marine Transportation

Seaborne freight is the primary means of transporting Japan's huge volume of raw-material imports and finished-good exports. Of the 133 designated "important ports," 21 have been classified as "specific important ports" for promotion of foreign trade; these include the Tokyo Bay area (Tokyo, Yokohama, Kawasaki, and Chiba), Nagoya, the Osaka Bay area (Osaka and Kobe), Kita Kyushu, and Wakayama Shimotsu (a major oil port).

Japanese shipping companies have lost international competitiveness because of rising wages and the continuing high value of the yen since 1985. By 1995 the total gross tons of vessels flying the Japanese flag had fallen about 49 percent from its peak of 39 million tons in 1980.

■Air Transportation

As of January 2001 there were 74 airlines in Japan, eight of which—including Japan Airlines Co., Ltd. (JAL) and All Nippon Airways Co., Ltd. (ANA)—operate scheduled international flights. Following the

The Shibaura waterfront district of Tokyo.

Passenger and Freight Transportation

(billions of passenger-kilometers)

Passenger	1970	1980	1990	1999
JNR/JR	189.7	193.1	237.7	240.8
Private railways	99.1	121.4	149.8	144.3
Automobiles and buses	284.2	431.7	853.1	955.6
Air	9.3	29.7	51.6	79.4
Passenger ships	4.8	6.1	6.3	4.5
Total	587.2	782.0	1298.4	1424.5

(billions of ton-kilometers)

Freight	1970	1980	1990	1999
Rail freight	63.4	37.7	27.2	22.5
Automobiles	135.9	178.9	274.2	307.2
Freight ships	142.5	222.2	244.6	229.4
Air	0.1	0.3	0.8	1.0
Total	341.9	439.1	546.8	560.2

Source: Ministry of Land, Infrastructure and Transport.

implementation of airline industry deregulation measures, in 1998 Skymark Airlines Co., Ltd., and Hokkaido International Airlines Co., Ltd. (AIR DO) became Japan's first new airlines in 35 years. Their low price policies spurred competition in the airline industry.

In 2000 Japan had 93 commercial and semicommercial airports, 60 of which had facilities for passenger jet aircraft. The country's major international airports are New Tokyo International Airport (Narita), Tokyo International Airport (Haneda), Osaka International Airport, and Kansai International Airport.

Mass Communications

The spread of democratic institutions, university education, and urban lifestyle in the 20th century created enormous markets for newspapers, magazines, books, and electronic media. Article 21 of the Constitution of Japan guarantees freedom of speech and the press and prohibits censorship.

■Newspapers

Newspapers covering domestic news were first started by the

Japanese in 1868. The two principal newspaper categories in Japan today are nationwide newspapers, which include the five major dailies, and local newspapers, which include the many newspapers focused on a given prefecture or region. There are also sports, evening, community, and English-language newspapers. Japan's two news agencies, Kyodo News Service and Jiji Press, primarily support the local press since the nationwide papers rely mainly on their own news bureaus.

The five major daily general papers in order of circulation are: *Yomiuri shimbun*, *Asahi shimbun*, *Mainichi shimbun*, *Nihon keizai shimbun*, and *Sankei shimbun*. They maintain their own nationwide home-delivery networks. The total circulation (with morning and evening editions counted as one subscription) of daily papers in October 1998 was 53.67 million, or an average of 1.16 newspapers per Japanese household. More than 90 percent are delivered directly to homes.

■Broadcasting

In 1926 the Japan Broadcasting Corporation (NHK) was granted a radio broadcasting monopoly under the firm control of the Ministry of Communications. In 1950 the Broadcasting Law made provision for a commercial sector and reorganized NHK as a strictly public service organization. Television broadcasting started in 1953.

Japan's broadcasting system consists of two types of broadcast enterprise: NHK and the various commercial companies. As a special

©NTV

A television program recording studio at Nippon Television Network Corporation (NTV).

corporation, NHK is neither a state-operated enterprise nor a public corporation. In contrast to commercial broadcasting, which operates on advertising revenue, NHK receives 98 percent of its financing from reception fees paid by television set owners.

Analog-format terrestrial (as opposed to satellite) television broadcasts are still the standard in Japan. However, the government is promoting an early shift to digital broadcasting as part of efforts to achieve consistency among terrestrial broadcasting, satellite broadcasting, and cable transmissions.

Terrestrial Broadcasting: NHK conducts nationwide and local broadcasts through two television, one FM radio, and two AM radio channels. It also conducts international broadcasts (Radio Japan) in 22 languages throughout the world. Commercial television broadcasting consists of five networks: NNN (Nippon Television Network Corporation [NTV]), JNN (Tokyo Broadcasting System, Inc. [TBS]), FNN (Fuji Telecasting Co., Ltd.), ANN (Asahi National Broadcasting Co., Ltd.), and TXN (Television Tokyo Channel 12, Ltd.). Digital terrestrial broadcasts of television and radio are to be introduced gradually between 2003 and 2006.

There are two major commercial AM radio broadcasting networks: the Japan Radio Network and the National Radio Network. Commercial FM broadcasting is dominated by the Japan FM Broadcasting Association, which operates a nationwide network with FM Tokyo as its key station.

Satellite Broadcasting: Full-scale NHK BS broadcasts began in 1989 with two channels. In 1991 Japan's first commercial satellite broadcasting channel, called WOWOW, was introduced. In December 2000 BS digital broadcasts began with 10 television channels as well as radio and data transmission channels. Analog format communications satellite (CS) broadcasts began in 1992. Digital CS broadcasts were started by PerfecTV (now SKY PerfecTV) in 1996.

Information Communications

Japan's information communications systems have been riding a wave of revolutionary change since the mid-1990s as a result of the drastic advances being made in information technology (IT). In addition to transforming the structure of business and industry, rapid expansion of the use of the Internet and mobile communications is having a major effect on the lifestyles of the Japanese people. The government has been implementing deregulation measures in order to introduce market principles into Japan's telecommunications field, and thereby increase the competitiveness of Japanese companies in the global market. An early step in this direction was the privatization of the government-run telephone-service monopoly in 1985 to create Nippon Telegraph and Telephone Corporation (NTT). In 1999 NTT was reorganized as a holding company overseeing two regional telephone companies and one long-distance telephone company. The number two general telecommunications company in Japan, now known as KDDI Corporation, was created in August 2000 when two new common carriers merged with KDD Corporation, the company which up until 1985 held a monopoly on international telephone services in Japan. Deregulation has brought many new companies into Japan's information communications market, including major foreign firms.

The mobile communications market in Japan got its start with the introduction of car telephone services in 1979. With rapid developments in technology reducing the size and weight of portable telephones while increasing their functional capabilities, the market exploded in the mid-1990s, and in 1999 the number of contracts for mobile telephone services surpassed the number for fixed-location telephone services. Also in 1999, NTT DoCoMo and a number of other companies introduced services enabling portable telephone users to access information and execute transactions (purchase books, make plane reservations, etc.) via Internet web sites.

The second half of the 1990s saw rapid growth in Internet use among the general public. The number of users as of the end of 2000 was estimated at about 47 million, a 74-percent increase over the previous year. A considerable portion of this drastic growth resulted from the rapid increase in the use of portable telephones and mobile terminals for Internet access. In wire-based Internet access, Japan in 2001 entered a full-scale broadband era with the rapid spread of the use of DSL (digital subscriber lines), ADSL (asymmetric DSL), and cable Internet services offering flat-rate continuous connections.

In November 2000 the government passed a law that seeks to help Japan deal with the radical social and economic changes resulting from the IT revolution. Among the objectives of this law are: building of an ultra-high-speed network infrastructure, promotion of electronic commerce, protection of the information of individual citizens, facilitation of equal access to IT resources, and realization of an "electronic government." In the building of the network infrastructure, the private sector is to play the lead role, with the government working to create an environment of free and open competition.

©Kyodo

A Tokyo shop selling portable telephones, including new types which can access the Internet.

融

Harmony

Pure clear water fills the stone basin called the *tsukubai*.
The tea ceremony guests take up the ladle and lightly
rinse their hands and mouths. This ritual serves to cleanse them
of mundane concerns so they can enter into an idealized
environment of harmony and respect for people and objects.
With its careful attention to cleanliness and order,
the tea ceremony strives to bring peace to body and spirit.

Culture and Life

巧

Some of the most technologically sophisticated inventions of the Edo period (1600–1868), mechanical dolls called *karakuri ningyo* moved with the help of cables, springs, pulleys, and wooden gears. When pointed in the right direction, this tea-bearer doll will carry a cup of tea to a guest and return with the empty cup.

Religion

Religious life in Japan is rich and varied, with a long history of interaction among a number of religious traditions, including Shinto, Buddhism, Confucianism, and Christianity. Article 20 of the Constitution of Japan states that freedom of religion is guaranteed to all.

The worship of *kami*, the Shinto gods, slowly emerged at the dawn of Japanese history and crystallized as an imperial religious system beginning in the Nara period (710–794). The only major religion indigenous to Japan, Shinto can be seen both as a loosely structured set of practices and attitudes rooted in local communities and as a strictly defined and organized religion at the level of the imperial line and the state. After the Meiji Restoration of 1868 Shinto became the state religion, but it lost this official status after World War II. Many local Shinto shrines hold annual festivals, and customs such as visiting a shrine (or Buddhist temple) on New Year's Day and taking newborn babies to the local shrine are still observed across Japan.

Buddhism was introduced from Korea in the mid-6th century and spread quickly among the ruling aristocracy. Prince Shotoku gave imperial support to the building of major temples, including Horyuji in present-day Nara Prefecture. Zen Buddhism, which came to be favored by the dominant military class, arrived from China in the 12th century, and around the same time popular sects such as the Pure Land sect also emerged. Today Buddhism is divided into 13 principal sects maintaining about 80,000 temples. Buddhist rites are used in about 90 percent of the funerals held in Japan.

Jesuit missionaries brought Christianity to Japan in the mid-16th century, but in the next century the Tokugawa government proscribed the religion and expelled all missionaries. Christianity was reintroduced into Japan in the Meiji period (1868–1912).

In the 20th century a large number of new religions have developed,

Left: Considered one of the most important Shinto shrines, Izumo Shrine is located in the town of Taisha in Shimane Prefecture. The god of Izumo has traditionally been regarded as the god of marriage, good fortune, and agriculture.
Right: The five-storied pagoda of the temple Horyuji in Nara Prefecture. Built in the 7th century, it is the oldest pagoda in Japan.

with some attracting huge numbers of followers. The teachings of these religions are in many cases primarily Buddhist or Shinto in origin, but elements of Confucianism, Taoism, and shamanism are also sometimes present.

Festivals and Annual Events

Japanese festivals, holidays, and other ceremonial occasions fall into two main categories: *matsuri* (festivals) and *nenchu gyoji* (annual events).

■Festivals

Matsuri are chiefly of sacred origin, related (at least originally) to the cultivation of rice and the spiritual well-being of local communities. They derive ultimately from ancient Shinto rites for the propitiation of the gods and the spirits of the dead, and for the fulfillment of the agricultural round. Thus, Japanese *matsuri* are synchronized with seasonal changes and are classified according to the four seasons.

A *matsuri* is basically a symbolic act whereby participants enter a state of active communication with the gods (*kami*); it is accompanied by communion among participants in the form of feast and festival. In

Japanese Festivals

① Kamakura Festival
② Omizutori
③ Aoi Festival
④ Sanja Festival
⑤ Nebuta Festival
⑥ Kanto
⑦ Nagasaki Suwa Festival (Okunchi)
⑧ Tori no Ichi
⑨ Chichibu Festival

A Calendar of Japanese Festivals

Month	Date	Event	Location
January	7	Dazaifu Usokae	Dazaifu Shrine, Dazaifu, Fukuoka Prefecture
	9–11	Toka Ebisu	Imamiya Ebisu Shrine, Osaka
	14–15	Niino Snow Festival	Izu Shrine, Anan, Nagano Prefecture
	15	Wakakusayama Turf Burning	Nara, Nara Prefecture
	20	Motsuji Madarajin Festival	Motsuji, Hiraizumi, Iwate Prefecture
February	early February	Sapporo Snow Festival	Sapporo, Hokkaido
	15–16	Kamakura Festival	Yokote, Akita Prefecture
	17–20	Hachinohe Emburi	Hachinohe, Aomori Prefecture
March	12–13	Omizutori	Todaiji, Nara, Nara Prefecture
	13	Kasuga Festival	Kasuga Shrine, Nara, Nara Prefecture
April	14–15	Takayama Festival	Hie Shrine, Takayama, Gifu Prefecture
May	early May	Ombashira Festival	Suwa Shrine, Suwa, Nagano Prefecture
	3–4	Hakata Dontaku	Fukuoka, Fukuoka Prefecture
	3–5	Hamamatsu Festival	Hamamatsu, Shizuoka Prefecture
	15, alternate years	Kanda Festival	Kanda Shrine, Tokyo
	15	Aoi Festival	Kamo Shrine, Kyoto
	third weekend	Sanja Festival	Asakusa Shrine, Tokyo
June	first Sunday	Mibu no Hanadaue	Chiyoda, Hiroshima Prefecture
	7–16, alternate years	Sanno Festival	Hie Shrine, Tokyo
	17	Saikusa Festival	Isakawa Shrine, Nara, Nara Prefecture
July	17	Gion Festival	Yasaka Shrine, Kyoto
	23–25	Soma Nomaoi Festival	Ota, Nakamura, and Odaka shrines, Fukushima Prefecture
	24–25	Tenjin Festival	Temmangu, Osaka
	last Sunday	Peiron Boat Race	Nagasaki, Nagasaki Prefecture
August	1–7	Nebuta Festival	Aomori and Hirosaki, Aomori Prefecture
	4–7	Kanto	Akita, Akita Prefecture
	12–15	Awa Dance	Tokushima, Tokushima Prefecture
September	16	Tsurugaoka Hachimangu Yabusame	Tsurugaoka Hachiman Shrine, Kamakura, Kanagawa Prefecture
October	7–9	Nagasaki Suwa Festival (Okunchi)	Suwa Shrine, Nagasaki, Nagasaki Prefecture
	22	Kurama Torch Festival	Yuki Shrine, Kyoto
November	2–4	Karatsu Kunchi (Karatsu Festival)	Karatsu Shrine, Karatsu, Saga Prefecture
	2 or 3 days at 12-day intervals	Tori no Ichi	Otori shrines throughout Japan
December	3	Chichibu Festival	Chichibu Shrine, Chichibu, Saitama Prefecture
	17	Kasuga Wakamiya Grand Festival	Kasuga Wakamiya Shrine, Nara, Nara Prefecture
	31	Okera Festival	Yasaka Shrine, Kyoto

a broad sense, *matsuri* may also include festivals in which the playful element and commercial interests have all but obliterated the original sacramental context.

■Annual Events

Nenchu gyoji are annual and seasonal observances, many of Chinese or Buddhist origin. They are arranged seasonally to form an annual calendar of events and tend to be observed by families or communities throughout Japan at about the same time. The term *nenchu gyoji* was first used in the Heian period (794–1185) to refer to the imperial court calendar.

National Holidays

① First shrine visit of the year on New Year's Day.

② People praying and offering donations on their first temple or shrine visit of the new year.

Month	Date	Holiday
January	1	New Year's Day (Ganjitsu)
	2nd Monday	Coming-of-Age Day (Seijin no Hi)
February	11	National Foundation Day (Kenkoku Kinen no Hi)
March	around 21	Vernal Equinox Day (Shumbun no Hi)
April	29	Greenery Day (Midori no Hi)
May	3	Constitution Day (Kempo Kinembi)
	5	Children's Day (Kodomo no Hi)
July	20*	Marine Day (Umi no Hi)
September	15*	Respect-for-the-Aged Day (Keiro no Hi)
	around 23	Autumnal Equinox Day (Shubun no Hi)
October	2nd Monday	Sports Day (Taiiku no Hi)
November	3	Culture Day (Bunka no Hi)
	23	Labor Thanksgiving Day (Kinro Kansha no Hi)
December	23	Emperor's Birthday (Tenno Tanjobi)

*From 2003, the third Monday of the month.

Annual Events

① Bean-Scattering Ceremony.

② Bon dance performed as part of the Bon Festival.

Month	Date	Event
January	1–3	New Year's days (Sanganichi)
	7	Seven Herb Festival (Nanakusa no Sekku)
February	3 or 4	Bean-Scattering Ceremony (Setsubun)
	8	Needle Memorial Service (Hari Kuyo)
March	3	Peach Festival (Momo no Sekku); also called Doll Festival (Hina Matsuri) and Girl's Festival
	17–24	Spring *higan* (seven-day Buddhist memorial service)
April	8	Flower Festival (Hana Matsuri; celebration of the birth of Śākyamuni)
May	5	Tango Festival (Tango no Sekku); also called Boy's Festival and designated a national holiday as Children's Day
July	7	Tanabata Festival (Tanabata); also called Star Festival
	13–15	Bon Festival (Urabon'e, honors the spirits of ancestors, held in August in some areas)
September	9	Chrysanthemum Festival (Kiku no Sekku; also called Choyo no Sekku)
	17–20	Autumn *higan*
November	15	"Seven-Five-Three" Festival (Shichigosan)
December	31	New Year's Eve (Omisoka)

Many Heian-period annual events of Chinese origin developed into folk traditions and are still observed today. Chief among these are the five *sekku* (seasonal festivals), one example being Tango no Sekku (Tango Festival).

After the Heian period, events manifesting values of the warrior class also developed. Thus a heterogeneous body of *nenchu gyoji*, modified and expanded in the practice of the Edo-period (1600–1868) townsmen, has been transmitted to the present day. An example is the observance known as Shichigosan (Seven-Five-Three), which derives from court observances in which rites of passage were performed for boys of three and five years and girls of three and seven years.

Japanese Language

The native language of the overwhelming majority of the more than 100 million inhabitants of the Japanese archipelago.

Although the Japanese and Chinese languages are entirely unrelated genetically, the Japanese writing system derives from that of Chinese. Chinese characters were introduced sometime in the 6th century, if not before, and the modern writing system is a complex one in which Chinese characters (*kanji*) are used in conjunction with two separate phonetic scripts (*hiragana* and *katakana*) developed from them in Japan. Japanese has also absorbed loanwords freely from other languages, especially Chinese and English, the former chiefly from the 8th to the 19th century and the latter in the 20th century.

There seems to be a growing consensus among Japanese scholars that syntactically Japanese shows an Altaic affinity, but that at some time in its prehistory it received an influence in vocabulary and morphology from the Malayo-Polynesian languages to the south.

For each syllable, the *hiragana* character is shown above and the *katakana* character below.

The Japanese Syllabaries

n	wa	ra	ya	ma	ha	na	ta	sa	ka	a
ん ン	わ ワ	ら ラ	や ヤ	ま マ	は ハ	な ナ	た タ	さ サ	か カ	あ ア
	ゐ ヰ	り リ	い イ	み ミ	ひ ヒ	に ニ	ち チ	し シ	き キ	い イ
	ゐ ヰ i	り ri リ	い i イ	み mi ミ	ひ hi ヒ	に ni ニ	ち chi チ	し shi シ	き ki キ	い i イ
	う ウ u	る ル ru	ゆ ユ yu	む ム mu	ふ フ fu	ぬ ヌ nu	つ ツ tsu	す ス su	く ク ku	う ウ u
	ゑ ヱ e	れ レ re	え エ e	め メ me	へ ヘ he	ね ネ ne	て テ te	せ セ se	け ケ ke	え エ e
	を ヲ o	ろ ロ ro	よ ヨ yo	も モ mo	ほ ホ ho	の ノ no	と ト to	そ ソ so	こ コ ko	お オ o

The Japan Book

Japanese Literature

Japanese literary art has received foreign influences since its beginning. Before the middle of the 19th century, the source of influence was the culture of China. After the middle of the 19th century, the impact of modern Western culture became predominant.

■Early and Heian Literature

The *Kojiki* (712, Record of Ancient Matters) and the *Nihon shoki* (720, Chronicles of Japan), the former written in hybrid Sino-Japanese and the latter in classical Chinese, were compiled under the sponsorship of the government for the purpose of authenticating the legitimacy of its polity. However, among these collections of myths, genealogies, legends of folk heroes, and historical records there appear a number of songs—written with Chinese characters representing Japanese words or syllables—that offer insight into the nature of preliterate Japanese verse.

The first major collection of native poetry, again written with Chinese characters, was the *Man'yoshu* (late 8th century; tr *The Ten Thousand Leaves*), which contains verses, chiefly the 31-syllable *waka*, that were composed in large part between the mid-7th and mid-8th centuries. The earlier poems in the collection are characterized by the direct expression of strong emotion but those of later provenance show

©Kyoto National Museum

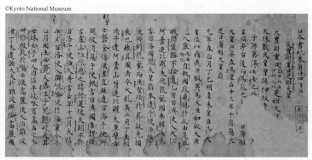

A section from one of the 31 volumes of the *Nihon shoki*, the oldest official history of Japan. Completed in 720, the *Nihon shoki* covers events from the mythical age of the gods up to the reign of Empress Jito, which ended in 697. Kyoto National Museum. National Treasure.

the emergence of the rhetorical conventions and expressive subtlety that dominated the subsequent tradition of court poetry.

A revolutionary achievement of the mid-9th century was the development of a native orthography (*kana*) for the phonetic representation of Japanese. The system contributed to a deepening consciousness of a native literary tradition distinct from that of China. The *Kokin wakashu* (905, Collection of Japanese Poems from Ancient and Modern Times), the first of 21 imperial anthologies of native poetry, was assembled in the early 10th century.

The introduction of *kana* also led to the development of a prose literature in the vernacular, early examples of which are the *Utsubo monogatari* (late 10th century, Tale of the Hollow Tree), a work of fiction; the *Ise monogatari* (mid-10th century, Tales of Ise), a collection of vignettes centered on poems; and the diary *Tosa nikki* (935; tr *The Tosa Diary*). From the late 10th century the ascendancy of the Fujiwara regents resulted in the formation of literary coteries of women in the courts of empresses. These women produced great prose classics, such as the *Genji monogatari* (early 11th century; tr *The Tale of Genji*), a fictional narrative by Murasaki Shikibu, and the *Makura no soshi* (996–1012; tr *The Pillow Book of Sei Shonagon*), a collection of essays by Sei Shonagon.

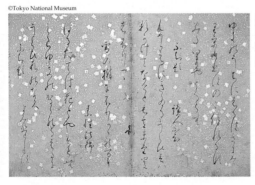

A portion of the oldest extant full copy of the 10th-century *Kokin wakashu* poetry anthology. 12th century. Tokyo National Museum. National Treasure.

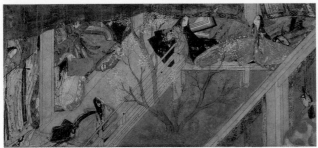

An illustration from a 12th-century scroll painting portraying scenes from the 11th-century novel *The Tale of Genji*. Written by court lady Murasaki Shikibu, this work has been called the first great novel in world literature. Here a courtier is shown trying to catch a glimpse of two court ladies. Tokugawa Art Museum. National Treasure.

©Tokugawa Art Museum

■Medieval Literature

The chief development in poetry during the medieval period (mid-12th–16th centuries) was linked verse. Arising from the court tradition of *waka*, *renga* (linked verse) was cultivated by the warrior class as well as by courtiers, and some among the best *renga* poets, such as Sogi, were commoners. A major development in prose literature of the medieval era was the war tale. The *Heike monogatari* (ca 1220; tr *The Tale of the Heike*) relates the events of the war between the Taira and Minamoto families that brought an end to imperial rule. The social upheaval of the early years of the era led to the appearance of works deeply influenced by the Buddhist notion of the inconstancy of worldly affairs (*mujo*). The theme of *mujo* provides the ground note of the *Heike monogatari* and the essay collections *Hojoki* (1212; tr *The Ten Foot Square Hut*) by Kamo no Chomei and *Tsurezuregusa* (ca 1330; tr *Essays in Idleness*) by Yoshida Kenko.

■Edo Literature

The formation of a stable central government in Edo (now Tokyo), after some 100 years of turmoil, and the growth of a market economy led to the development in the Edo period (1600–1868) of a class of wealthy townsmen. Literary works became marketable commodities, giving rise to a publishing industry. Humorous fictional studies of contemporary society such as *Koshoku ichidai otoko* (1682; tr *The Life of*

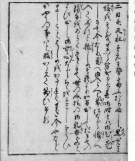

Illustration and text pages from a copy of *The Life of an Amorous Man,* a late-17th-century prose work by Ihara Saikaku. A picaresque account of the amorous adventures of its hero Yonosuke, it is the first example of the *ukiyo-zoshi* (tales of the floating world) genre. Waseda University Library.

©Waseda University Library

an Amorous Man) by Ihara Saikaku were huge commercial successes, and prose works, often elaborately illustrated, that were directed toward a mass audience became a staple of Edo-period literature.

The 17-syllable form of light verse known as *haikai* (later known as *haiku*), whose subject matter was drawn from nature and the lives of ordinary people, was raised to the level of great poetry by Matsuo Basho.

■Modern Literature

The Meiji Restoration of 1868 was followed by the wholesale introduction of Western technology and culture, which largely displaced Chinese culture. As a result the novel became established as a serious and respected genre of the literature of Japan. A related development was the gradual abandonment of the literary language in favor of the usages of colloquial speech, fully achieved for the first time in *Ukigumo* (1887–1889, Drifting Clouds) by Futabatei Shimei. Although the *tanka* (a 31-syllable poem) and the *haiku* remained viable poetic forms, a genre of free verse developed under the influence of Western poetry. Early stylistic influences on Japanese literature were romanticism, introduced in the 1890s by novelist Mori Ogai, and naturalism, out of which developed the enduring genre of the confessional novel (I-novel or *watakushi shosetsu*).

In addition to Ogai, major writers of the early part of the century include Natsume Soseki, who brought the Japanese realistic novel to full maturity, and short-story writer Akutagawa Ryunosuke. Many of the works of the later writers Nagai Kafu, Tanizaki Jun'ichiro, and Kawabata Yasunari take an elegiac view of Japanese life before its transformation by Western influences. Kawabata was awarded Japan's first Nobel Prize in literature in 1968.

Writers whose work was strongly influenced by Japan's defeat in World War II include Dazai Osamu, Ibuse Masuji, and Ooka Shohei. After the 1950s Japanese fiction can no longer be easily characterized in terms of the early postwar consciousness; important writers of this period include Abe Kobo, Mishima Yukio, Endo Shusaku, and Oe Kenzaburo, winner of the Nobel Prize for literature in 1994. In the last decades of the 20th century, young writers such as Murakami Ryu, Murakami Haruki, and Yoshimoto Banana were writing in a style that had more in common with their counterparts abroad than with Japanese writers of an earlier era.

① Futabatei Shimei
② Mori Ogai
③ Natsume Soseki
④ Akutagawa Ryunosuke
⑤ Kawabata Yasunari
⑥ Oe Kenzaburo

Japanese Art

Over the centuries, a wide variety of social, economic, political, cultural, and environmental factors have had an influence on the development of Japanese art. The temperate climate and four distinct seasons provided an abundance of seasonal symbols and motifs, such as the plum, the cherry, the maple, and the chrysanthemum, which appear again and again in Japanese art. The influence of China and Buddhism was particularly strong in the premodern period, and since the mid-19th century Western art and techniques have had a significant effect on traditional aesthetics.

Painting

Japanese painting is characterized by a wide range of styles in a wide array of formats, from horizontal and hanging scrolls to album leaves, fans, walls, and free-standing and sliding screens. The themes of Japanese painting range from the elegant images of the court and Buddhist institutions to the more common and accessible realities of

©Museum of the Imperial Collections, Sannomaru Shozokan

This six-panel folding screen, titled *Chinese Lions*, is the work of 16th-century Kano school painter Kano Eitoku, who is believed to be the first painter to introduce the dramatic use of fields of gold leaf in large mural compositions. Museum of the Imperial Collections, Sannomaru Shozokan.

An ink painting (ca 1501) by Sesshu Toyo, this landscape scroll titled *Amanohashidate* depicts the famous scenic spot of that name. Kyoto National Museum. National Treasure.

©Kyoto National Museum

genre scenes. Until the 19th century, China was the principal source of innovation.

■Premodern Painting

Buddhist Painting (Butsuga): With the introduction of Buddhism and Buddhist culture from Korea and China in the 6th century, the production of Buddhist paintings as religious icons and temple decorations began. In the Heian period (794–1185), which is considered the golden age of Buddhist painting, the rise of Esoteric Buddhism led to the development of mandala painting, and the spread of Pure Land Buddhism spurred the development of the new genre of *raigozu*, depictions of the Buddha Amida arriving to welcome the dying to paradise.

Scroll Painting (Emakimono): The painting of these long horizontal hand scrolls containing illustrations, often with accompanying text, flourished in the Heian period and Kamakura period (1185–1333). Frequently used to illustrate a literary work, such as *The Tale of Genji*, or the history of a temple or shrine, *emakimono* sets varied from 1 or 2 rolls to as many as 48.

Ink Painting (Suibokuga): Ink painting is a monochrome style of painting characterized by the use of black ink (*sumi*). It was first introduced from China in the 8th century, but it was not widely seen in

Japan until the 14th century, when it became popular in the great Zen monasteries. In the 15th century Zen monk painters developed a Japanese style of ink painting as an expression of Zen spirit, and ink painting became the mainstream of Japanese painting. Later ink painting was gradually secularized and separated from Zen Buddhism, and it continued to develop as a vibrant medium throughout the Edo period (1600–1868).

Screen and Wall Painting (Shoheiga): A grandiose polychrome style developed in the late 16th century for paintings executed on the walls and sliding and folding screens of traditional Japanese-style buildings. Used to decorate the many castles being built in the Azuchi-Momoyama period (1568–1600), screen and wall paintings with backgrounds sprinkled with gold dust or covered with wafer-thin gold leaf became prominent. (See Ukiyo-e.)

■Modern Painting

After the Meiji Restoration of 1868, political and social change was effected in the course of a modernization campaign by the new government. Western-style painting was promoted officially, and a number

In this Japanese-style modern painting titled *Muga* (Innocence), artist Yokoyama Taikan uses an innocent child to represent the Zen concept of enlightenment. 1897. Tokyo National Museum.

of painters traveled abroad for study under government auspices. However, the initial burst of enthusiasm for Western art soon yielded to renewed appreciation of traditional Japanese art. Japanese-style painting (*nihonga*) regained prominence in the late 19th century, although some *nihonga* artists also showed Western influence in their treatment of space and light and their abandonment of outline in polychrome paintings.

Although new styles such as impressionism, surrealism, and abstractionism were adopted, prior to World War II only a few artists managed to succeed in surmounting the largely derivative character of Western-style painting in Japan. In the postwar-period, however, Japanese painters have emerged as significant contributors to international movements in art.

Ukiyo-e

A genre of art, chiefly in the medium of the woodblock print, that arose early in the Edo period (1600–1868) and built up a broad popular market among the middle classes. In the late 19th century *ukiyo-e* prints had a profound influence on the paintings of French impressionists such as Vincent van Gogh and Claude Monet. Subject matter tended to focus on the brothel districts and the *kabuki* theaters, and formats ranged from single-sheet prints to albums and book illustrations. *Ukiyo-e* flourished throughout Japan, attaining their most characteristic form in the prints produced in Edo (now Tokyo) from about 1680 to the 1850s. Kitagawa Utamaro achieved a heightened closeness to his subjects by using the format of the *okubi-e* or bust portrait. Utamaro's women are often sensuous, even sensual, to an extreme. Katsushika Hokusai developed a style that was highly individual, combining Chinese and Western influences with elements drawn from the native

Beneath the Wave off Kanagawa, a woodblock print from Hokusai's most famous series, *Thirty-Six Views of Mt. Fuji*. Tokyo National Museum.

©Tokyo National Museum

tradition. His series of landscape prints *Thirty-Six Views of Mt. Fuji* had begun to appear by 1831. He was also a prolific draftsman who employed a variety of techniques to create the astounding array of images in his famous 13-volume *Hokusai manga* (1814–1849, Hokusai's Sketches). Hokusai's only true rival in landscape was Ando Hiroshige, whose *The Fifty-Three Stations of the Tokaido Road* series brought him fame and a host of imitators.

Buddhist Sculpture

Buddhist sculpture was introduced to Japan from China and Korea, and from the 6th through the 8th century Japanese Buddhist sculpture closely followed continental prototypes. A more native style did not evolve until the 9th century.

Most early sculpture was rendered in gilt bronze or wood. Continental models provided the stylistic framework for much of the sculpture produced for Asuka-period (593–710) temples. Important examples of early Buddhist sculpture include the gilt-bronze Shaka

Triad (dated 623) and the wood Guze Kannon at the temple Horyuji in Nara Prefecture.

After the capital at Heijokyo (present-day Nara) was built and occupied in 710, inaugurating the Nara period (710–794), much sculpture was commissioned for the various temples being constructed in and around the new city. Although bronze remained an important medium, more works were rendered in clay and in "dry" lacquer techniques.

Important works of the 8th century preserved in the Nara region include the gilt-bronze Yakushi Triad (the Buddha Yakushi flanked by two bodhisattvas) at Yakushiji and the hollow-lacquer Rushana at Toshodaiji. The construction of Todaiji initiated another wave of sculpture commissions, assigned to a government-sponsored workshop. The principal Todaiji project was the development of the colossal gilt-bronze Rushana that became known as the Great Buddha of Nara, a sculpture some 16 meters (53 ft) in height.

By the end of the 8th century, with the move of the capital from Nara to Heiankyo (present-day Kyoto) and the start of the Heian period (794–1185), wood had emerged as the favored medium for sculpture and was to remain so through the modern era. At first most sculptures were carved from one large block of wood, but by the 11th

This gilt-wood statue of
the Buddha Amida was completed
by the sculptor Jocho in 1053.
In the Phoenix Hall at
the temple Byodoin near Kyoto,
it is one of the earliest extant works using
the full-blown joinery method.
National Treasure.

century, as demand for sculpture increased, joinery (joined-woodblock construction) was the preferred—and more efficient—method.

The Heian period saw the emergence of Buddhist monk-sculptors and sculptor lineages as an artistic and economic force in Kyoto and Nara. Important works of the early Heian period include the 9th-century wood sculpture of Yakushi at Jingoji in Kyoto and the group of 9th-century wood sculptures, arranged in the form of a mandala, at Toji in Kyoto. One of the most influential late-Heian works is the gilt-wood sculpture of the Buddha Amida at Byodoin near Kyoto.

The Kei school, a 12th-century lineage of sculptors, produced key artists, among them Unkei and Kaikei, who would define sculpture in the Kamakura period (1185–1333). Wood remained the favored medium and joinery the technique, but, in contrast to the Heian tendency to gild statuary, Kamakura-period sculptors also showed much interest in paint as a finish for sculptures. Kaikei's 13th-century figure of the bodhisattva Jizo, originally at Todaiji, is an example of this tendency. In addition, the eyes of the sculpture have been inlaid with crystal in the "jewel eyes" technique, which was developed late in the 12th century and became a standard feature in the increasingly "realistic" forms of Kamakura-period sculpture.

Sculpture after the Kamakura period tended to become increasingly standardized, with sculptors producing works largely limited to conventional modes.

Ceramics

Ceramics in Japan has a long history, stretching over 12,000 years. In the development of ceramic materials, China was the great innovator, and all of Japan's advanced technology came directly from there or indirectly by way of the Korean peninsula; more often than not, China

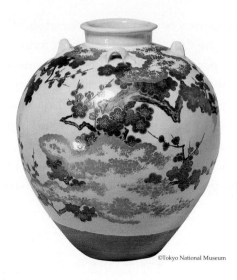

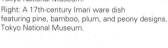

Left: This tea-leaf storage jar by 17th-century artist Nonomura Ninsei features stylized representations of plum blossoms. Tokyo National Museum.

Right: A 17th-century Imari ware dish featuring pine, bamboo, plum, and peony designs. Tokyo National Museum.

©Tokyo National Museum

©Tokyo National Museum

also set the style. Yet also typical of Japan's attitude toward ceramics was the fact that, while newer wares representing advanced technology might be accorded a position of highest status, they by no means obliterated existing wares and techniques, which for the most part continued unaffected. As a result, Japanese ceramics became steadily richer in variety, and the ceramic articles produced in Japan today cover the full range from earthenware directly descended from neolithic precedents to the most demanding Chinese-style glazed wares.

In the mid-17th century a crucial influence was added in the form of the European market, which gave special preference to an Arita-produced decorated ware called Kakiemon ware. The second half of the 17th century saw the full flowering of such decorated wares. Colorful Imari ware and Kakiemon ware were shipped to Europe from Kyushu in great quantities. In Kyoto, a popular form of decorated earthenware or stoneware known as *kyo-yaki* was developed. Only isolated ventures, such as Kutani ware, attempted the production of porcelain in competition with the dominant kilns in Arita.

Contemporary Japanese ceramics may be said to have begun shortly after 1900 with the emergence of the "studio potter" with an individual name and style. The studio potter of the 20th century came to ceramics by choice rather than by birth, and the typical eclectic style was based on a strong knowledge of Japanese ceramic history. From 1926, the folk crafts movement began to foster interest in the aesthetic value of traditional craftwork and skillfully made simple objects of daily use—among them ceramics. Mashiko (Tochigi Prefecture) is famous as a center of folk-style pottery. Many foreign potters have studied in the town.

Gardens

Japanese gardens possess a unique beauty derived from the combination and synthesis of various elements. There is a compositional beauty derived from a blending of natural plantings, sand, water, and rock, made unique by the natural beauty of Japan's landscape and seasonal change, and a symbolic beauty arising from the expression of Shinto beliefs and Buddhist intellectual conventions. It has been said that the use of groupings of rocks is a distinguishing feature of the Japanese garden and provides its basic framework. The ancestors of

The Zen-style dry landscape garden at the temple Ryoanji in Kyoto. Surrounded by a low wall on three sides, it consists of only 15 oddly shaped rocks of varying sizes placed on a bed of white gravel.

The Shokintei teahouse is located in one of the tea gardens of the Katsura Detached Palace, a 17th-century imperial villa in Kyoto.

the modern Japanese referred to places surrounded by natural rock as a "heavenly barrier" or "heavenly seat," believing that gods lived there. The first gardens amidst the mountains of Yamato imitated ocean scenes with large ponds rimmed by wild "seashores" and dotted with islands.

In the Heian period (794–1185) the gardens of the palatial mansions of the aristocracy featured narrow streams that passed between the buildings. The ponds were of simple shape yet were large enough for boating, and the large area between the main buildings and the pond was covered with white sand and used for formal ceremonies.

With the rise of the cult of the Buddha Amida in the 10th century, a garden style modeled on the image of the Pure Land, as described in scripture and religious tracts, was developed.

The Muromachi period (1333–1568) has been called the golden age of Japanese gardens. Skilled groups of craftsmen were active, and new waterless rock and sand gardens were created under the influence of Zen Buddhist doctrine.

The tea ceremony emphasized a quiescent spirituality, and this was reflected in the tea garden through which one approached the tea-house. Among the contributions of the tea garden to the contemporary

Japanese garden are stepping-stones, stone lanterns, and groves of trees, as well as stone washbasins and simply constructed gazebos for guests being served tea.

During the Edo period (1600–1868) a synthesis of preceding forms took place. The garden of the Katsura Detached Palace in Kyoto is an example of the "many-pleasure" style, which became fully established in the mid-Edo period.

Flower Arrangement

Japanese flower arrangement (*ikebana*) had its origin in early Buddhist flower offerings and developed into a distinctive art form from the 15th century, with many styles and schools. The attention given to the choice of plant material and container, the placement of the branches, and the relationship of the branches to the container and surrounding space distinguished this art from purely decorative uses of flowers.

The style known as *rikka* ("standing flowers"), the oldest style of flower arrangement, prized sophisticated arrangements that sought to reflect the majesty of nature. Complex symbolism from Buddhist cosmology attached to each of seven branches.

In the late 16th century, a new form of flower arrangement called

©Ikenobo

An *ikebana* class.

nageire ("to throw or fling into") emerged for use in the tea ceremony. The late 17th century saw the emergence of the *shoka* or *seika* ("living flowers") style, basically consisting of three main branches arranged in an asymmetrical triangle. The ideal in *shoka* was to convey the plant's essence and its natural line of growth.

In the late 19th century, there was a revival of *ikebana* when Ohara Unshin introduced his *moribana* ("piled-up flowers") style, which stressed color and natural plant growth, utilizing low arrangements that nearly touched the sides of shallow containers.

In the postwar era, avant-garde *ikebana* revolutionized the materials considered acceptable. Not only live flowers and grasses but also plastic, plaster, and steel are used to express surrealistic and abstract concepts in the arrangements. Today, there are approximately 3,000 *ikebana* schools in Japan. The most popular styles are the Ikenobo, Ohara, and Sogetsu.

Tea Ceremony

A highly structured method of preparing powdered green tea in the company of guests. It is the culmination of a union of artistic creativity, sensitivity to nature, religious thought, and social interchange.

Early in the Kamakura period (1185–1333), the Japanese priest Eisai returned from Buddhist studies in China, bringing the tea ritual practiced in Chinese Buddhist temples during the Song dynasty (960–1279).

In Sakai, south of Osaka, there was a group of wealthy merchants, which espoused a modest manner of tea drinking. Out of this tradition came Takeno Joo, who taught a sensitive connoisseurship and the aesthetic sensibility known as *wabi*, which cultivates a simple and austere type of beauty. His influence was widely felt but was most important

A tea ceremony guest drinking from an individually prepared bowl of *usucha* (thin tea).

in his instruction of his student Sen no Rikyu. Substituting common Japanese-made objects for the rare and expensive Chinese tea utensils used previously, Rikyu transformed the tea ceremony and perfected it as a vehicle for expressing *wabi*.

There were many masters of tea, with heirs and followers who eventually gathered into schools. Ura Senke and Omote Senke are the leading schools in Japan today, both were founded by descendants of Rikyu.

A full tea presentation with a meal is called a *chaji*, while the actual making of the tea is called *temae*. A simple gathering for the service of tea may be called a *chakai*. The selection of utensils is determined by time of year, season, and time of day or night, as well as special occasions such as welcoming someone, bidding farewell, a memorial, a wedding, flower viewing, and so on.

The tea is prepared and served in a specially designated and designed room, the tearoom. It is devoid of decoration with the exceptions of a hanging scroll and flowers in a vase. The scroll provides the appropriate spiritual atmosphere for serving tea. Flowers for tea are simple, seasonal, and seemingly "unarranged."

During the ceremony two types of tea are served. The *koicha* (thick tea), made by adding a very small amount of hot water to the powdered tea, is prepared by the host in a single bowl from which all guests drink. The *usucha* (thin tea) is served individually.

Japanese Cooking

There are three fundamental types of traditional full-course Japanese cuisine: *honzen ryori*, an assembly of dishes served on legged trays at formal banquets; *chakaiseki ryori*, a series of dishes sometimes served before the tea ceremony; and *kaiseki ryori*, a series of dishes for parties, often served at restaurants specializing in Japanese cuisine. Other types

Popular Japanese Foods

① *Sukiyaki*: Thinly sliced beef, vegetables, *tofu*, and other ingredients cooked at the table in a large skillet or iron pot in a broth of soy sauce, *mirin* (sweet *sake*), and sugar.

② *Udon*: Type of wheat-flour noodle. Served in a variety of ways, both cold and hot (shown here).

③ *Soba*: Type of noodle primarily made from buckwheat flour. Served in a variety of ways, both cold (shown here) and hot.

④ *Sushi*: Vinegared rice topped or combined with such items as raw fish, shellfish, or cooked egg.

⑤ *Tempura*: Fresh fish, shellfish, or vegetables dipped in a batter (*koromo*) of flour mixed with egg and water and then deep-fried.

are *osechi ryori*, dishes traditionally served on important holidays such as New Year's, and *shojin ryori*, Buddhist vegetarian dishes.

A characteristic of Japanese cuisine is the emphasis placed on seasonal awareness; for example, glass and bamboo tableware are considered appropriate for summer. The main ingredients in Japanese cooking are seafood, vegetables, and rice. The consumption of raw seafood has long been a distinguishing feature of native cuisine. Because of the abundance of foods supplied by the seas surrounding Japan and the influence of Buddhism, which militated against the killing of animals, Japanese cooking formerly made little use of the flesh of animals and fowl, dairy products, and oils and fat. Principal seasonings are fermented products of soybeans, such as soy sauce and *miso* (soybean paste), or of rice, such as *sake*, vinegar, and *mirin* (sweet *sake*). To preserve the natural flavors of ingredients, strong spices are avoided in favor of milder herbs and spices.

Traditional Architecture

Traditional residential architecture in Japan is perhaps best viewed as a response to the natural environment. Traditional Japan was a primarily agricultural society, centering on activities associated with rice planting. A feeling of cooperation, rather than an antagonistic relationship, developed between the Japanese and their natural surroundings. Instead of resistance or defense, accommodation and adaptation became the basic stance. Traditional Japanese architecture is characterized by the same attitude toward the natural environment, responding in particular to climatic and geographical conditions.

Japan's climate is distinguished by hot, humid summers and cold, dry winters, and the Japanese house has evolved accordingly to make the summers more bearable. The traditional Japanese house was raised

A traditional-style house (*minka*) with a thick thatched roof.

slightly off the ground and the interior opened up to allow for unrestricted movement of air around and below the living spaces. Associated with the heat and humidity of summer were sun and frequent rain. This necessitated a substantial roof structure with long, low overhangs to protect the interior.

The development of the individual spaces within the house was a gradual process of breaking down the larger open space that was available into smaller, more human-scaled spaces. Individual rooms were later defined by *shoji* and *fusuma* (sliding doors) that could still be removed to form a single large space. The choice of building materials has been determined by the climate, wood being preferred to stone. Wood responds more sensitively to the climate, being much cooler and absorbing moisture in summer and not as cold to the touch in winter. Wood is also more suited to withstand earthquakes, frequent occurrences in Japan.

Modern Architecture

Following the Meiji Restoration of 1868, the government invited foreign engineers and experts to train Japanese and oversee initial construction projects.

After World War I architects from Europe and the United States contributed to the reevaluation of traditional Japanese architecture. The renewed interest in tradition led to the development by Yoshida Isoya of a new style in residential architecture that assimilated traditional *sukiya-zukuri* techniques.

One of the best-known and most influential modern Japanese architects is Tange Kenzo. He developed a methodology linking Japanese traditional elements with the achievements of science and technology in architectural form and established his reputation with a number of dramatic buildings in the 1950s and 1960s, including the Yoyogi National Stadium (1963) built for the 1964 Tokyo Olympics.

The 1970s saw a reevaluation of architectural priorities, led by Isozaki Arata. Rejecting the tendency toward the total commercialization of architecture and construction, Isozaki argued that architecture had to regain its independence from commercial and technological imperatives. It was about this time that architects who regarded themselves primarily as artists began to make their appearance, among the most distinguished being Ando Tadao.

Designed by Tange Kenzo and located in Shinjuku Ward, the Tokyo Metropolitan Government Offices were completed in 1991.

The demand of business for imposing buildings reasserted itself in the 1980s, but architects responded with buildings that incorporated more artistic design features. Tange Kenzo's Tokyo Metropolitan Government Offices (1991) are a good example of the monumental style that resulted.

Traditional Theater

The five major genres of Japanese traditional theater, all still in performance, are *bugaku*, No, *kyogen*, *bunraku*, and *kabuki*.

Among the five, *bugaku* stands apart as a ceremonial dance associated only with court ritual, in which the theatrical element is minimal and music predominates. *Bugaku* incorporates aesthetic and structural principles current in the 8th century—admixtures of Central Asian, Indian, and Korean elements assimilated by China and adopted by Japan during a period of cultural borrowing.

No, *kyogen*, *bunraku*, and *kabuki*, by contrast, are indigenous forms representing successive periods of political and social change in Japan. All adhere to Asian dramatic principles emphasizing symbolism and allusive imagery, as opposed to the Aristotelian concept of mimesis, the imitation of reality, which dominates Western dramatic theory.

■No

The world's oldest extant professional theater, No is a form of musical dance-drama originating in the 14th century. It was developed into basically the same form performed today by the great actors and playwrights Kan'ami and his son Zeami. Under the patronage of Muromachi *shogun* Ashikaga Yoshimitsu, Zeami refined the Kanze style of performance based on Zen artistic principles of restraint, economy of expression, and suggestion rather than statement.

No masks, which are usually worn only by the main character

A scene from the No play *Izutsu* (The Well Curb) by Zeami.

©National No Theater

(known as the *shite*), are categorized into general types, such as young woman or demon. In many plays the *shite* changes masks midway through, with the second mask revealing the character's true nature. The staccato music of the flute and drum players and the chanting of the chorus enhance the feeling of *yugen* (mystery and depth) created by the No performance.

In 2001 UNESCO proclaimed Nogaku theater (No and *kyogen*) as being one of the "masterpieces of the oral and intangible heritage of humanity."

■Kyogen

The comic interludes that are an integral part of No performance, *kyogen* pokes fun at human frailties as did the traditional Asian story-tellers, jesting at social pretensions, marital discord, quackery, and so forth.

■Bunraku

Bunraku has a unique place in the theater world of Japan, where puppet performance has been accepted as the equal of orthodox drama. The performance is a composite of four elements: the puppets, the movement of the puppets, the vocal delivery by the chanter, and the

A scene from the *kabuki* play *Shibaraku* (One Moment). A historical play written by Ichikawa Danjuro I, it is shown here being performed by Ichikawa Danjuro XII in 1996.

©Shochiku

musical accompaniment by the 3-stringed *shamisen*. Each puppet of a major character is operated by three men.

■Kabuki

One of Japan's major genres of traditional theater, *kabuki* began in the early 17th century as a kind of variety show performed by troupes of itinerant entertainers. By the beginning of the Genroku era (1688–1704), there had developed three distinct types of *kabuki* performance: *jidai-mono* (historical plays); *sewa-mono* (domestic plays), which usually portrayed the lives of the townspeople; and *shosagoto* (dance pieces). The tastes of the prosperous merchant culture of the Edo period (1600–1868) can be seen in the magnificent blend of playacting, dance, and music of *kabuki*, and in its emphasis on both the exploits of flamboyant heroes and the travails of ordinary people trying to reconcile human desire and social duty. Primarily an actor's theater, some of the greatest stars of *kabuki* are the *onnagata*, male actors playing female roles. *Kabuki* can also be considered a modern theater form because many new plays have been written for it over the last century. It remains extremely popular, with performances playing to full theaters in Tokyo and elsewhere.

Modern Theater

In the Meiji period (1868–1912) a number of modern theater genres were born. *Shimpa* (new school), which developed in the 1890s, was a genre similar to *kabuki* in its acting methods; *shimpa*, however, utilized actresses (*kabuki* remained all male) and was more open to outside influence. *Shingeki* (new theater), a movement that began at the turn of the 20th century, was stimulated by Ibsen, Shakespeare, and other Western (mainly naturalist and romantic) playwrights. A number of prominent Japanese playwrights and novelists have written for the *shingeki* stage.

The underground theater movement called the *shogekijo undo* (little-theater movement) emerged in the 1960s. The movement based itself in small theaters, and performances were also staged in tents or open-air settings. Rebelling against the limitations of established theater, the *shogekijo undo* troupes experimented with the structure of plays, the emotive aspect of acting, and the use of theatrical space. They soon overtook *shingeki* to become the new center of contemporary theater in Japan.

A noteworthy tendency in the Japanese theatrical world since the 1980s has been the great popularity of American and British musicals.

©Disney

A scene from the Shiki Theatre Company production of the musical *The Lion King*.

In addition to revivals of older Broadway hits, many new musicals such as *Cats* and *Les Miserables*, have also been performed in Japanese-language versions. Many original Japanese works have also been produced.

Rakugo

Popular form of comic monologue in which a storyteller (*rakugoka*) creates an imaginary drama through episodic narration and skillful use of vocal and facial expressions to portray various characters. The storyteller, dressed in a plain *kimono*, crosses to stage center and seats himself on a cushion before his audience, with a hand towel and a fan as his only props. There he remains until he has delivered his final line, usually a punning punch line (*ochi*). This is the characteristic ending from which the term *rakugo* was coined.

Traditional Music

The traditional history of Japanese music normally starts with the Nara period (710–794). Japanese music had its roots in the music of

A *koto* performance with *shakuhachi* (bamboo flute) accompaniment.

Buddhism and the vibrant traditions of Tang dynasty (618–907) China. Chinese and Korean courts or monasteries were the sources and models of most of the music in Japanese courts and temples but, because of the international dynamism of continental Asia from the 7th through the 10th century, influences from South and Southeast Asia can be found as well. The instrumental (*kangen*) and dance (*bugaku*) repertoires of the court, generically known as *gagaku*, reflect such origins in their classification into two categories: *togaku*, pieces derived from Chinese or Indian sources, and *komagaku*, music from Korea and Manchuria.

During the turbulent change from a court-dominated to a military-dominated culture at the end of the 12th century, more theatrical genres of music became popular. The *biwa* (lute) of the court became the accompaniment not only of itinerant priests and evangelists but also of chanters who recited long historical tales, particularly the *Heike monogatari*. The 13-stringed *koto* (zither) was used for ancient courtly solo and chamber music and continued to develop in the 16th century, primarily in the mansions of the rich or in temples. By the 17th century quite different *koto* pieces appeared. The end-blown *shakuhachi* (bamboo flute) also developed new schools of performance and repertory during this period, but it is the three-stringed plucked lute (*shamisen*) that best represents the new musical styles and new audiences of the 16th through the 19th century. By the 18th century the narrative tradition of the puppet theater (*bunraku*) had become a major source of literature, which was performed by skilled chanters (*tayu*) with *shamisen* accompaniment. The *kabuki* theater adopted some of this material for its own plays, but it also developed a combination of other genres of *shamisen* music plus the percussion and flute ensemble (*hayashi*) of the No. In the 19th century, compositions using theatrical genres and instruments but intended for dance recital or purely concert performances appeared.

Modern Music

■Western Classical Music

Today Western classical music flourishes in Japan. In quantity and quality of composition, performance, music education, and audience appreciation, Japan bears comparison with Western nations. The history of Western-classical-music study and performance in Japan is a relatively short one, however, beginning with the government's efforts to import Western music following the Meiji Restoration of 1868.

In 1887 the government established the Tokyo School of Music (now Tokyo University of Fine Arts and Music), Japan's first official school of music. Japan's oldest symphony orchestra, the New Symphony Orchestra, was formed in 1926 and began giving performances in 1927. In 1951 it was renamed the NHK Symphony Orchestra and is considered Japan's leading orchestra.

The New National Theater, which opened in 1997, contains a hall especially for opera performances. As of 2001, the Association of Japanese Symphony Orchestras had 23 professional orchestras as members. There are also many Japanese musicians active in the international music scene. Ozawa Seiji has been music director of the

©The New Japan Philharmonic

The New Japan Philharmonic.

Boston Symphony Orchestra since 1973, and in 2002 he is to become the music director of the Vienna State Opera. Pianist Uchida Mitsuko and violinist Goto Midori are both top international performers. Composer Takemitsu Toru had a considerable reputation as a major figure in international contemporary music.

■Popular Music

Japanese popular music in the 20th century developed through the combination of traditional Japanese melodies with the rhythms and instruments of Western popular music. The oldest popular genre still around today is *enka*, which tends to be sentimental, bittersweet, nostalgic songs of love lost. Sung in a slow vibrato, *enka* still has many dedicated fans and is the mainstay of *karaoke*, prerecorded musical accompaniment to which people sing along.

In the 20th century Japanese popular music was influenced by a diverse range of imported genres. Jazz and blues were especially popular in the 1920s, and since the 1960s strong influence has been felt from a succession of pop genres (rock and roll, heavy metal, funk, rap, ethnic music, reggae, hiphop, etc.) which now make up a significant share of the Japanese market. Since the mid-1990s the term "J-Pop" has come to be used to refer to all Japanese popular music genres except *enka*. A number of J-Pop artists have become very popular with young people throughout East Asia.

In *karaoke* performances like the one pictured here, people sing along to prerecorded musical accompaniment.

Instrumental music of both Western instruments (pianos, guitars, synthesizers, etc.) and traditional Japanese instruments (*shamisen*, *shakuhachi*, *taiko* drums, etc.) arranged in a modern style has also become quite popular. Prestigious international music awards have been won by electronic music composer and musician Kitaro and composer and musician Sakamoto Ryuichi, who is well known for his soundtrack compositions.

Japanese Film

Motion picture production in Japan began around 1899. Until the coming of talkies, which did not become the major portion of production until 1936, movies in Japan were accompanied by a *benshi*, a live performer who sat by the side of the screen and orally interpreted the images of the film. From its silent film era, Japanese film has been divided into two main genres: the *jidaigeki* (period films that generally featured swordplay) and *gendaigeki* (films with modern settings).

The decade of the 1950s, apart from being the most prosperous in the history of the Japanese cinema, is considered by many to be its creative Golden Age. When Kurosawa Akira's innovative *jidaigeki Rashomon* (1950) won the top prize at the Venice Film Festival in 1951, it opened the Japanese cinema to international audiences. Kurosawa's style alternated between such social issue–oriented *gendaigeki* as *Ikiru* (1952, To Live) and such seminal *jidaigeki* epics as *Shichinin no samurai* (1954, Seven Samurai).

Mizoguchi Kenji and Ozu Yasujiro, two established directors from the prewar period, produced some of their greatest work in the 1950s. Mizoguchi refashioned the historical film with such exquisite works as *Ugetsu monogatari* (1953, Ugetsu). In *Tokyo monogatari* (1953, Tokyo Story) Ozu Yasujiro concentrated on the emotional complexities of

① Kurosawa Akira
② Ozu Yasujiro
③ Imamura Shohei

middle-class family life. In 1954 the major studio Toho created Japan's first film monster in *Gojira* (Godzilla).

In the 1960s many people purchased their first television and stopped going to the movies, where attendance plummeted from the all-time high of 1.1 billion in 1958 to 300 million in 1968. Half of the movie theaters in the country closed during the 1960s.

The dominant director of the 1970s was a major-studio man, Yamada Yoji. His overwhelmingly popular success was the *Torasan* series (formal series title *Otoko wa tsurai yo* [It's Tough Being a Man]). These films fused the two bedrock motifs of Japanese film: the everyday collective life of a family and the adventures of a lonely wanderer.

In the 1990s Japanese films again attracted attention abroad. In 1997 *Unagi* (1997, Eel) by Imamura Shohei became the second film by that director to win the Cannes Film Festival Grand Prize, the first being *Narayama-bushi ko* (1983, The Ballad of Narayama). In the same year *HANA-BI* (1997, Flower and Fire) by Kitano Takeshi won the Venice Film Festival Grand Prize. In the second half of the 1990s a changing of the guard appeared to be taking place in Japanese cinema with the appearance of new directors such as Iwai Shunji, who directed *Love Letter* (1995), and Suo Masayuki, who directed *Shall We Dance?* (1996).

■**Animated Films**

Some of the most popular Japanese-made films released since the 1960s have been animated films. Although his work appeared more on television than in theaters, leading comic-strip author Tezuka Osamu

Tetsuwan Atomu (Astro Boy).

©Tezuka Productions

pioneered the field in 1963 when he began making the animated serial *Tetsuwan Atomu* (1963, Astro Boy) based on one of his comic-book serials.

Japan's premier animated-film director in the late 20th century was Miyazaki Hayao, who combined uninhibited humor, social criticism, and poetic lyricism in works such as *Tonari no Totoro* (1988, My Neighbor Totoro) and *Mononoke Hime* (1997, The Princess Mononoke).

Japanese Clothing

The international recognition accorded Japan's top fashion designers, coupled with a relatively affluent economy at home, have sparked an interest in fashion among Japanese consumers. In fact, Japan has become one of the world's major retail markets for designer wear—both domestic and imported.

Western-style apparel was first introduced to Japan during the Meiji period (1868–1912), when the country ended its long isolation and began to open up to American and European cultural influences. While many men quickly adopted Western clothing, it was not until after World War II that large numbers of Japanese women abandoned *kimono* in favor of the more practical styles worn by Westerners. Nowadays, most women don *kimono* only on special occasions, and men do so even less frequently.

The luxurious fabrics and sophisticated motifs used for *kimono* continue to inspire some of Japan's leading couturiers, while others are striking out in new directions. Drawing upon a rich textile heritage, designers like Mori Hanae, Miyake Issei, and Kawakubo Rei are able to infuse their fashions with a distinctly Japanese flavor.

But fashionable clothing is by no means the rule in Japan. For millions of people—schoolchildren, department store employees, and taxi drivers—daily attire is a uniform of one sort or another. Together with their stylishly clad compatriots, these people in regulation attire contribute to the lively pastiche that characterizes contemporary Japanese dress.

Traditional Sports and Martial Arts

With its origins in tests of strength performed in Shinto rituals during Japan's prehistoric period, *sumo* matches came to be held as part of

©The Japan Sumo Association

A *sumo* match between the two *yokozuna* Takanohana (left) and Musashimaru at the tournament held in November 2000.

imperial court ceremonies beginning from around the 8th century. *Sumo* has been a professional sport since the early Edo period (1600–1868). In addition to watching *sumo* matches, imperial courtiers in the Heian period (794–1185) and later practiced falconry and *kemari*, a game in which players form a circle and kick a ball back and forth without letting it fall to the ground.

The origins of modern Japanese martial arts can be found in fighting techniques that developed in the Muromachi period (1333–1568), examples include *kenjutsu* (fencing; present-day *kendo*), *jujutsu* (present-day *judo*), and *kyujutsu* (archery; present-day *kyudo*). Skill in these martial arts were of life and death importance to the warriors of the time, and many schools developed with their own characteristic techniques. After the end of widespread military conflicts in the Edo period, the martial arts lost some of their practical importance, and the mental and spiritual aspects of training were increasingly emphasized.

Following the Meiji Restoration (1868), modern Western sports, such as baseball and track and field events, were introduced from the United States and Europe, and interest in martial arts training declined. However, reflecting the growing nationalism and emphasis on military strength, martial arts such as *kendo* and *judo* became a part of military training and were added to school curriculums in the early decades of the 20th century. After World War II martial arts training was banned for a time on the grounds that it encouraged militarism, but *kendo* and

©Kodokan

Left: A *judo* practice session.
Right: A *kendo* practice session.

judo, as well as *sumo*, reappeared in school physical education programs in the 1950s, and in 1964 *judo* was made an official Olympic event at the Tokyo Olympics.

■Judo

A form of unarmed combat that stresses agile motions, astute mental judgment, and rigorous form rather than sheer physical strength. *Judo* techniques include throwing, grappling, and attacking vital points. The first two techniques are used in competition, but the third is used only in practice.

■Kendo

Japanese fencing based on the techniques of the two-handed sword of the *samurai*. The weapon is a hollow cylinder made of four shafts of split bamboo. Fencers' faces are protected by a face mask; the trunk of the body is protected by a chest protector. Training is based on a variety of movements of attack and defense. Most fundamental are stance, footwork, cuts, thrusts, feints, and parries.

■Karate

Art of self-defense that uses no weapons and relies instead on three main techniques: arm strikes, thrusts, and kicks. A distinction is made between offensive and defensive techniques, which are modified according to the position of one's opponent. For defense, there are various parrying methods corresponding to each of the methods of offense.

■Sumo

A 2,000-year-old form of wrestling that is considered by many to be the national sport of Japan. *Sumo* became a professional sport in the early Edo period (1600–1868), and although it is practiced today by amateur wrestlers, it has its greatest appeal as a professional spectator sport.

The object of this sport is for a wrestler to force his opponent out of the *dohyo* (center circle of the elevated cement-hard clay ring) or cause him to touch the surface of the *dohyo* with any part of his body other than the soles of his feet. The actual conflict is often only a matter of seconds. To decide who has stepped out or touched down first is often extremely difficult and requires the closest attention of a referee, dressed in the court costume of a 14th-century nobleman, on the *dohyo* and judges sitting around the *dohyo* at floor level.

The Japan Sumo Association officially lists 82 winning techniques consisting of assorted throws, trips, lifts, thrusts, shoves, and pulls. Of these, 48 are considered the "classic" techniques but the number in actual daily use is probably half that.

Unique to *sumo* is the use of a belly band or belt called a *mawashi*. Most *sumo* matches center on the wrestler's attempts to get a firm, two-handed grip on his opponent's *mawashi* while blocking the opponent from getting a similar grip on his.

Tournaments lasting 15 days are held every other month. Professional *sumo* wrestlers are ranked in a pyramid, rising from beginners at the bottom to grand champions (*yokozuna*) at the top.

Modern Sports

Sports and sports-related activities are extremely popular in Japan. Most secondary schools and universities provide facilities for team sports, and many large companies encourage and support sports activities for their employees. In addition, professional spectator sports draw large crowds. Modern Western-style sports, including baseball, soccer, gymnastics, tennis, and winter sports, were first introduced during the Meiji period (1868–1912) by foreign teachers.

Today the most popular leisure sports in Japan are baseball, tennis, swimming, skiing, golf, jogging, and fishing. Professional sports in Japan include baseball, *sumo*, soccer, boxing, tennis, and golf, baseball and *sumo* being the most popular. Since 1912 Japan has participated in such international events as the Asian Games and the Olympic Games, hosting the 1964 Tokyo Olympic Games, the 1972 Sapporo Winter Olympic Games, and the 1998 Nagano Winter Olympic Games. In total Japanese athletes have won 98 gold, 97 silver, and 104 bronze medals in the Summer Olympics (1896–2000), and 8 gold, 9 silver, and 12 bronze medals in the Winter Olympics (1924–1998).

©Kyodo

① A Japan Professional Football League (J. League) soccer game between the Yokohama F. Marinos and the Kashima Antlers in 2000.
② Professional baseball player Matsuzaka Daisuke instructing young players in 2000.
③ The start of the annual Tokyo-Hakone *ekiden kyoso* (long-distance relay race) in 2000. In this race university teams run from Tokyo to Hakone and back.

©Kyodo

©Kyodo

Internet Information Resources

A wide range of statistical and other information about Japan is available on the English language pages of the Internet sites of various Japanese-government organizations. Many of these sites have link collections pointing to the others. Several good entry points are given below along with a short description of some of the information available.

■ Prime Minister of Japan and His Cabinet (http://www.kantei.go.jp/foreign/index-e.html)
   Extensive information on the prime minister and cabinet. The "Links to Ministries and Other Organizations" entry on the links page displays an organization chart with links to all government ministries, etc.

■ Ministry of Foreign Affairs (http://www.mofa.go.jp)
   Extensive information on Japan's foreign policy, economic affairs, and regional affairs. Description of Japan's visa requirements. Links to other government information, tourist information, cultural information, etc.

■ Ministry of Public Management, Home Affairs, Posts and Telecommunications
   (http://www.soumu.go.jp/english/index.html)
   Extensive information on the many areas under this ministry's jurisdiction. The "Statistics" link on the main page displays the Statistics Bureau and Statistics Center page, which provides access to the *Statistical Handbook of Japan* and a wide variety of other statistical material.

■ Japan Information Network (http://jin.jcic.or.jp)
   This site is a gateway for a wide variety of information on Japan. It includes an extensive graphical and text database concerning Japan's economy, society, culture, and traditions.

■ Economic and Social Research Institute (http://www.esri.cao.go.jp/index-e.html)
   The site of this institute, which is part of the Cabinet Office, presents a variety of statistical and policy information. The SNA (National Accounts) link (in the table of contents) presents Japan's gross domestic product (GDP) data.

Japanese Government White Papers and Annual Reports

The various ministries and agencies of the Japanese government prepare many white papers and other reports each year on a wide range of topics. Some of the reports for which a summary or the full text is available in English are shown below. Many of these are available on the Internet, but the addresses often change so links are not included here. The ministry or agency issuing the report is shown in parenthesis.

■ *Annual Report on Food, Agriculture, and Rural Areas in Japan* (Ministry of Agriculture, Forestry and Fisheries)
■ *Annual Report on Health and Welfare* (Ministry of Health, Labour and Welfare)
■ *Annual Report on Japanese Agriculture* (Ministry of Agriculture, Forestry and Fisheries)
■ *Annual Report on Japan's Economy and Public Finance* (Cabinet Office)
■ *Annual Report on the Promotion of Science and Technology* (Ministry of Education, Culture, Sports, Science and Technology)
■ *Annual Report on Trends of Forestry* (Ministry of Agriculture, Forestry and Fisheries)
■ *Diplomatic Blue Book* (Ministry of Foreign Affairs)
■ *Information and Communication in Japan* (Ministry of Public Management, Home Affairs, Posts and Telecommunications)
■ *Japanese Government Policies in Education, Science, Sports and Culture* (Ministry of Education, Culture, Sports, Science and Technology)
■ *Quality of the Environment in Japan* (Ministry of the Environment)
■ Summary of the *White Paper on Crime* (Ministry of Justice)
■ *Transport White Paper* (Ministry of Land, Infrastructure and Transport)
■ *White Paper on Labour* (Ministry of Health, Labour and Welfare)
■ *White Paper on International Trade* (Ministry of Economy, Trade and Industry)

Index

Page numbers in italics indicate entries that appear only in a caption, table, or graph, not in the main body of the text.